The Short and Tall of It

The Marvel of Our Existence is Incredible

by

Donna Lancaster

The Short and Tall of It
Copyright 2002 by Donna Lancaster

Editor-in-Chief -- Mindy F. Reed
Publisher-- Joan R. Neubauer
Cover Photo-- Tanya Sulak
Book Design and Printing-- Word Wright International

Printed in the United States of America

Library of Congress Cataloging-in-Publication Data

Lancaster, Donna.
The Short and Tall of it

p.   cm.

1. Physically handicapped--biography   2. Quality of Life 3.Handicapped--Attitudes

I. Title   II. Author   III. Biography   IV. Monograph

ISBN #0-9717868-0-1

HV 1552 LA   362.4309 LA   LC

The Short and Tall of It

by

Donna Lancaster

Cover design by
Stephen J. F. Neubauer

Word Wright International
P.O. Box 1785
Georgetown, Texas 78627
http://www.WordWright.biz

Printed in the United States of America.

Donna at five in 1938.

Dedicated to Life

Acknowledgements

My heartfelt thanks go to Tanya Sulak who has been my friend forever, through tall and short, and who has always believed in me. She knew when she could push me to write and wisely pulled back when I was stubborn, hardheaded and resisted writing another word. Her timely suggestions have greatly enhanced this book

I wish to thank my brother, Jack Hollingsworth, who has given me his solid support since the moment of my birth. He was always convinced that the book needed to be out there so others could experience this story.

Thanks to the remarkable men and women of Alcoholics Anonymous and Al-Anon. Their love and understanding have enriched my life beyond measure.

I want to thank my dear friend Barry Keenan, a fellow aspiring writer. He put me in touch with Mindy Reed, my editor and friend, who encouraged me to keep writing and lovingly cared for my manuscript.

I would like to thank my many friends who, to my surprise, never cared whether I was short or tall. Their support and encouragement were boundless.

Thanks also go to Joan R. Neubauer of Word Wright International for agreeing to publish my book. She patiently guided me and the manuscript through the tedious publishing process.

Thank you, Life, for inviting me to the Planet for this magnificent journey.

Introduction

Donna and I first met in 1982. In the years that followed, Donna and I became close in indescribable ways. Little did either of us know what a "ride" we were in for.

I've been interested in Donna's writing for the past 17 years and wanted her to share her story. At first she resisted. She couldn't see that her story was different from anyone else's. That's what makes Donna an exceptional person.

Every time I had been around Donna, she had worn her artificial legs and stood 5'8" tall. One day after moving to Whitney, she invited me to her home to visit. She answered the door without her "tall" legs. Even though I was surprised to see her 3'10" height, it was never uncomfortable, odd or not "normal" to me. It was natural.

As I observed Donna in her "short" world, I realized the hurdles she constantly overcame to accomplish the simple tasks of daily living, yet I never heard her complain. She took what was before her and conquered it with dignity and grace. No matter what her height, her stature is that of an enormous person.

Donna's life and the story you are about to read portray the journey of an individual who walks the walk, learns the lessons and as a result makes a contribution to life. I consider it a privilege and an honor to call her my friend. She and her story inspire me on a daily basis.

Donna is someone the light shines through. I hope your life is touched in a unique way as you experience this book, *The Short and Tall of It.*

Tanya Sulak

Chapter 1

Ideal: a picture in the mind, an illusion.

Donna June Hollingsworth was born on a hot June night in Kiowa, Kansas in 1932. Hospital deliveries were the exception then not the rule. So, Dr. Hammer and a nurse delivered the baby at the Hollingsworth's home. Ethel's pains, which had started early in the evening surprised her; the baby was not due for another month. Nevertheless, it was time and nothing would stop its arrival.

The glimpse of the newborn baby was a shocker. The legs were barely an inch long and the knees and lower legs were missing. The tiny, misshapen feet attached to the tiny legs had only four toes each. The little finger was missing from the left hand and the index and middle fingers were grown together. All of this in a package that weighed barely three pounds.

Virgil and Ethel were shocked. The pain of seeing their child in such a horribly deformed, physical body was almost unbearable. Time stood still. To look at the future was unthinkable.

Virgil and Ethel Hollingsworth had moved to Kiowa three years before. Although the Depression was in full swing, Virgil had a job with Sinclair Oil Company to deliver gasoline to wheat farmers in the area. Ethel was responsible for the care and raising of their two sons, Jack and Delbert, who were six and eight years old when Donna was born.

They had wanted a daughter.

But not this one.

Donna's bright smile and happy disposition helped to ease their anguish. Virgil could hold her in the palm of his hand and she fit nicely in his size 12 shoebox. Her legs were so short that her feet remained tucked inside her diaper. At first they didn't know if she'd live. With so many body parts missing, there might be internal problems that would be incompatible with life. Dr. Hammer had offered no promises. He did tell them though that she probably would never be able to walk because she had no hip joints to support her weight.

As the days passed, Ethel massaged Donna's legs hour after hour, perhaps hoping a miracle would happen. Maybe even the pressure of her hands would stimulate them to grow. Maybe it was desperation that made her do it, maybe hopelessness, maybe guilt. There is no way of knowing. One thing became certain to Ethel, her daughter, Donna, would be treated and cared for as any other "normal" child. They would never mention her differences. It would never be an issue or discussed with Jack and Delbert. With that decision, the whole family operated as though they were blind to Donna's handicap.

At the end of two months, Donna weighed five and a quarter pounds and measured seven and a half inches. By the time four months rolled around, she had grown to a happy, healthy, handful at eight and three-quarter pounds and ten and a half inches long. Concluding that Donna was a survivor, Dr. Hammer suggested that Virgil and Ethel take her to the Research Hospital in Kansas City for consultation. He said that the orthopedic specialists there might have a solution for her physical deformities.

It was four hundred miles from Kiowa to Kansas City. In 1932 there were no freeways or toll roads, some of the roads were not even paved. A neighbor, Anna, volunteered to keep Jack and Delbert so they wouldn't miss three days of school. Virgil serviced his gasoline delivery truck for the trip. Afraid, yet grasping for hope, with Donna on the seat between them, Virgil and Ethel headed for Kansas City.

After x-rays and examinations, the orthopedic specialists confirmed, that there were not enough bones in the right places to enable Donna to walk. The only possible solution would involve a series of operations grafting bones from Jack and Delbert into Donna, giving her the necessary bones to support walking.

Virgil and Ethel had many questions. Could Donna live through these long and involved operations? Would the bones removed from Jack and Delbert harm them in any way? Could any guarantee be given that the constructed legs would grow properly? How many operations would they have to perform? How long would Donna be in the hospital? And the big question: how much would it cost?

The doctors gave only vague answers. Absolute certainty was impossible. It would be an experiment. No promises. It was a tough decision. Ethel sensed that Donna's bright, brown eyes, dimpled smile and sunny disposition were bringing joy to the family. She could see a light and sparkle in her daughter, much more valuable than short, abnormal legs and an inability to walk. She needed to nurture this light and allow it to develop.

With her jaw set firmly, Ethel quietly answered the doctors, "No. We'll wait and see how Donna adjusts to her handicap. Later on she can make her own decision." A thread of hope had been dangled in front of her and she had courageously refused.

Having made the decision, they gathered Donna in their arms and headed back home to Kiowa. During the return trip, Ethel made a commitment, which she kept throughout her lifetime. She resolved to do everything possible, regardless of her own pain and overwhelming difficulties, to help Donna construct a self-sufficient life. Every decision would be based on one simple question, "What is best for Donna?" Her commitment was to be tested many, many times.

Chapter 2

What "is" is reality, what "ought to be" is illusion.

Life was simple, but not easy for the Hollingsworths in the early 1930s. Virgil had always worked hard and felt a tremendous responsibility to provide for his family. It was not popular for women to work outside the home so one salary provided all the basics. Ethel had taught school for two years before she married, but with Jack and Delbert, and now a child that required special attention, working out of the home was never even discussed.

Not long after the trip to Kansas City, Ethel and Virgil watched Donna pull herself along the floor with her arms. One day Ethel found her up on all fours like a puppy. She watched with apprehension as Donna began to climb and crawl over everything: chairs, couches, beds. The instinct to reach out and help Donna or stop her was powerful.

She squelched her impulse to scream, "Stop, you can't do that! Watch out! You'll fall and hurt yourself!" She had made the decision on the way back from Kansas City to do whatever was best for Donna. She had to control her instincts and impulses. As Donna climbed and crawled over everything in the house, Ethel remained silent. She was probably not aware of it, but the greatest gift she could and did give to Donna was to let her take charge of her own development and progress.

Acceptance did not come overnight. Gradually, Ethel learned to live in the moment, without feeling guilty for Donna's handicap or afraid for the future. She found Donna's bright mind and happy spirit delightful and entertaining. Love took the place of fear and guilt. It was not a self-seeking, possessive love, but a real concern that Donna would have every opportunity to be herself. Yes, it would have been easier if Donna had been so-called "normal." But, that was not the situation. She didn't like it, but not liking it wouldn't change it. Hopelessness gradually disappeared and Ethel and Virgil bravely accepted the hand that Fate had dealt them.

Ethel had just finished hanging the clothes on the line one spring day when Donna was about eleven months old. As she stepped through the door, carrying the empty basket, she suddenly stopped in disbelief. For a moment, she was transfixed. Shock, then amazement, swept over her. Donna was coming toward her, walking. She dropped the basket, scooped Donna into her arms and ran next door shouting to their neighbor, Anna.

"Donna can walk! Donna can walk! The doctors were wrong! She can walk!"

Up to this point they could not imagine a life for Donna without a wheelchair or someone to carry her. Inside, they harbored the thought that Donna's future could be one only of dependency. They would take care of her as long as they were able, but what about the time when they could not? How would she dress herself, go to the bathroom and what about school? To them, this miracle of walking was a giant step toward freedom and self-sufficiency. The whole family was ecstatic. However, they knew it would be inconvenient and frustrating to be only half as tall as everyone else. But, their outward determination became an inner belief. Donna wasn't handicapped, she was just put together a little differently.

Gradually, they became accustomed to her method of walking or running, wobbling like a duck on tiny feet. They spent many hours looking for her. She was either in the cabinets, under the bed or other pieces of furniture, in the clothesbasket, tucked neatly into a hole in a tree, or any of a hundred other places small and interesting to a curious child.

Ethel didn't stop Donna when she wanted to go outside and play with other children. Nor did she hesitate when it was time to march her off to kindergarten. She knew some kids would stare, make fun of her and call her names–but again and again, she remembered her commitment: "What is best for Donna?"

It was best for Donna to face the world and learn how to handle her own reactions to life's toughest lessons. Curious children were sometimes rude and cruel. Some called her "Wadley Duck." Others asked, "Why are you so little?" Donna patiently explained to them: "God made your legs long and He made mine short. That's all there is to it." This answer usually satisfied their curiosity and they accepted her as their friend and playmate.

Jimmy, who lived across the street, and Donna were sitting on the front steps one morning. Jimmy, also four years old, asked, "Donna, how come you're not tall like I am?"

Glancing at her short legs, she replied, "I'm not old enough, yet. When I grow up, I'll be tall."

Grown-ups were more self-conscious than children and were easily embarrassed. At times, when walking down the street, a child would point to Donna then say in a loud, clear voice which could be heard for three blocks, "Look Mommy, look at the little girl. She walks funny." The embarrassed mother would try to shut the child up and avoid eye contact. Donna would try to catch the mother's eye in order to send her a silent message, which said, "Don't be cross with him. I understand. It's okay."

Many other people, however, were kind and loving. The mailman, Gus, placed her carefully in his mailbag for the trip around the block. Her head was barely visible above the packages and letters. She felt like she was a "Special Delivery" package because none of her playmates would ever have this wonderful ride.

Virgil and Ethel treated her as they would any normal child. When she wanted a pair of roller skates, Virgil bought the smallest size he could find then adjusted them to the shortest position possible to fit her tiny feet. He buckled them around her crooked shoes and let her go. Of course, she fell many times, but since she didn't have far to fall, with practice, she soon made the linoleum floors her private skating rink.

She bragged to her friends, "I can skate under the kitchen table. I bet you can't do that."

When Ethel had tolerated it as long as she could, she deposited Donna outside to skate on the sidewalks. She would just have to learn to handle the cracks and rough spots! Roller-skating in the house was no longer permitted.

On her seventh Christmas, Santa Claus brought her a tricycle. Donna knew who Santa was, but Virgil was having so much fun, she didn't want to spoil it for him. He watched with fascination as she mounted up and tried the pedals. Her feet could not follow the pedals all the way around, so she pushed hard with one foot and waited for the other pedal to come around so she could push it with the other foot. Riding a tricycle soon became easy and she found the speed exhilarating. The basket on the front was just the right size for books or a loaf of bread. Her friends were traveling on bicycles, but for now, the tricycle was all she could handle. The bicycle would come later.

Frank and Anna were neighbors in Kiowa, and close friends to Virgil and Ethel. Anna, a nurse, gave Ethel comfort and hope during the somber days after Donna was born. Virgil had admitted to Frank early in Ethel's pregnancy, that he felt that something was terribly wrong. Around 1940, the Hollingsworth's moved back to South Haven, Kansas so they hadn't seen Frank or Anna for several years.

Early in 1942 Frank dropped by for a visit. As he stepped into the kitchen, Donna looked up and started to say, "Hi."

At the same moment, he glanced down at her and said, "Hi, midget."

Donna's insides crumbled. A huge lump had formed in her throat making it difficult for her to breathe. She swallowed several

7

times to keep from crying.

She ran out the back door, climbed into her favorite tree and sat for a long, long time in its protective branches. "I'm not a midget," she sobbed. "People must think I'm different, but I'm not. I'll show you that I'm not different." She made a vow. "No one will ever see me cry or hurt me again."

With intense determination, she joined in all the neighborhood games. In hopscotch, she couldn't jump far enough to miss the lines, but she didn't care. When she played jacks, it was awkward and almost impossible to hold the jacks in her left hand, but it didn't matter, she played the game the best she could. Hide and seek was a bit easier, because she could squeeze into hundreds of small spaces that were impossible for others. When she chose to hide, her friends almost never found her under the porch, in the neighbor's doghouse or in the washing machine. Drop the handkerchief was more difficult because she couldn't run very fast with her short legs. Her thoughtful friends chased her more slowly when she dropped the handkerchief behind them.

Did she feel lonely and isolated? No. Did she feel rejected? No. She was a part of whatever was taking place, and with little encouragement, took charge of whatever was happening.

The backyard was the neighborhood ball diamond, and of course, Donna was the catcher and team captain. The elm tree served as first base, the trash barrel, second, and the corner of the garage was third. The neighbor's strawberry patch was out of bounds. When it came time for Donna to bat, the pitcher tried to throw the ball somewhere between her shoulders and knees. Since she didn't have any knees, she usually made it to first base on walks.

The mid 1930s were a happy time. Donna had many friends. School was enjoyable and she made good grades. Virgil and Ethel never put her down or made her feel ugly, rejected or different. They did everything they could to help her feel good about herself. Jack and Delbert were supportive, as well. Six and eight years older, they were never embarrassed or ashamed to take her with them. And she was always ready to go to the Saturday afternoon movie with Jack and Delbert and their friends.

However, the late 1930s proved difficult for Virgil and Ethel. They had the financial stresses brought on by the Great Depression. Suddenly providing for the family as well as Donna's physical challenges became complicated and harder to manage. Because of his position as a "trouble-shooter" with the oil company, they moved often. In 1935, they moved from Kiowa, Kansas to Medicine Lodge. Then a few months later in 1935 they moved to Kingman and two years later to Wellington. In 1940 they made their final move to South Haven. Their attitude of not complaining but accepting made these changes and adjustments easier. Each house they lived in was clean and neat and nicely decorated. Ethel was a master at creating a pleasant environment. Certainly her parents had anxieties when Donna marched off to new schools in search of new friends. These experiences couldn't be faced for her, but Ethel could have freshly baked cookies waiting on the table when Donna and her brothers got home from school.

Chapter 3

Be grateful for pain.

South Haven, Kansas was a good final move because it was where Ethel and Virgil had been raised. Ethel and Virgil's parents were farmers and Jack and Delbert usually spent summers on their farms. A Derby service station lease was available on the main street, so Virgil went into the gasoline business for himself. South Haven, population 400, was in the middle of the finest wheat land in Kansas. The gasoline business was profitable. Then the war began.

Donna was lying on the couch near the radio when President Roosevelt announced that war had been declared. Three days earlier she had broken her leg. The trapeze rings on the school playground were the culprits. With her strong arms and adventuresome spirit, it didn't take much encouragement for her to swing freely from one ring to another. Her cousin, Sarah, had lifted her up to the rings. Suddenly, her hands slipped.

"Sarah, help me! I'm slipping!" she screamed. Sarah couldn't catch her before she fell with a thud to the ground. It didn't appear she was hurt, but she couldn't get up. The right leg had an ugly bend to it.

"Donna's hurt!" Sarah yelled. "Call Miss Patterson!"

The fourth grade teacher, Miss Patterson, hurried to the scene of the accident. She carefully picked Donna up and gently carried her to her car and laid her on the back seat. They drove to the doctor's office four blocks away. There were no tears, but Donna could hardly keep from vomiting. Someone called Ethel to come to the doctor's office.

The x-rays confirmed that the leg was broken just above the ankle. The doctor gave Donna an anesthetic, set the break and applied a cast. Usually when a cast is applied to a broken bone, it is necessary to include one joint above the break to ensure complete immobility. Since there were no such joints, the doctor insisted that she remain as motionless as possible for the next seven weeks. This was not an easy assignment for a healthy nine-year-old. So, there she was on the couch by the radio on December 7, 1941.

The September before Pearl Harbor Jack had just started to college at Kansas University in Lawrence. He knew that he would be drafted, so he finished one semester, then enlisted in the Army Air Corps. He had wanted to be a pilot, but the Air Corps had different plans for this highly intelligent young man. They trained him as a navigator. When he returned from England, after completing his missions, he became an Air Corps instructor. Delbert, a high school junior on December 7, 1941, finished school and, also, joined the Army Air Corps. He missed being a pilot by a few months. His happy-go-lucky nature and winning personality covered up his disappointment.

It seemed that everything was rationed: shoes, gasoline even groceries. Keeping Donna in shoes was a problem. Her right foot was smaller than her left one. When she walked, the right foot twisted, so the right shoe wore out quicker. Friends and neighbors gave Virgil and Ethel extra shoe stamps to keep Donna in shoes. Gasoline rationing had requirements. For every gallon of gasoline Virgil sold, he had to have a stamp for it. Virgil always had a few extra gasoline stamps and he gave them to servicemen who were traveling and didn't have enough stamps to make it home or make it back to their bases. Virgil felt if his sons were on the road and needed gasoline, he hoped that someone along the way would help them. After supper they sat around the kitchen table and licked gasoline stamps and put them in the books required by the government.

Around the house Ethel assigned Donna household chores. She had to keep her room clean and neat, do the dishes, set the table and carry out the trash. Ethel tried to maintain a delicate balance in her discipline and guidance. She was determined not to let Donna become spoiled and obnoxious.

After a supper of fried chicken, mashed potatoes and gravy, the dishes needed to be done because they used the kitchen table to lick and paste those stamps.

"Donna, it's time to do the dishes," Ethel said one day.

"I'm busy!" Donna called from the back bedroom.

"The dishes are to be done *now!*" she commanded.

Donna slowly inched her way into the kitchen, placed her stool in front of the sink and sullenly crawled up on it. Still pouting, she said, "The water is too hot and the dishes are greasy and messy."

Suddenly Ethel jerked her off the stool, slapped her across the face and said, angrily, "I'm tired of fooling with you. I'll do them myself."

Stunned, Donna couldn't believe her mother had slapped her. She had never seen her mother angry or upset. At that moment, Donna would have gladly washed a roomful of dishes. No doubt Ethel wondered if she had overreacted. She probably condemned herself and felt guilty for slapping Donna. But time proved that her choice of discipline was right on schedule. Donna needed to learn to accept responsibilities with a cheerful attitude. Whining and complaining would not be tolerated. The lesson was never forgotten.

చ చ చ

Designing clothes for Donna required some creative imagination. From the hips up, she was normal for her age. During the early years, Ethel made Donna sundresses or smocks with matching panties, always using bright, happy colors. She made no effort to cover up her short legs and crooked feet. Shoes that laced and reached above the ankle were easier to walk in than slippers. These high-top shoes gave her ankles more support and came almost to the hem of her dresses. At age three, it was okay for a girl's matching panties to show and everyone thought it was cute. But at age eleven, it was embarrassing.

At school she overheard a cutting remark by one of the boys, "I can see Donna's panties," he giggled.

Donna wanted to slap his face and rub his nose in the dirt. In dresses her panties showed, or they nearly reached the ground, so Donna started wearing slacks most of the time. She was more comfortable when she knew her bottom was covered.

"Riding a tricycle to school is silly," thought Donna. "All the other kids have bicycles. What I really need is a bicycle." She began begging her parents for one. They knew she couldn't ride a bike because she had no knees. What they didn't know was that she had dreamed, on three different occasions, that she was riding a bicycle. There was no doubt in her mind that she could do it. Finally, weary of her begging, they reluctantly consented.

Virgil purchased a second-hand, 16-inch girls' bicycle for fifteen dollars, from a local mechanic. He moved the seat back four inches, because she couldn't sit on the seat and pedal it at the same time.

Donna straddled the bicycle, put a foot on the pedal, then the other foot on the other pedal, and fell down. Time after time she fell, climbed back on, only to fall again. The gravel scraped her arms and legs. The concrete skinned her face and hands. Her back was bleeding from beating against the seat.

Finally, after three days, bloody and bruised, she and the bike managed to stay upright for a distance of thirty feet.

"I'm riding! it! I'm riding it! Whoopee!"

The bike tilted from side to side a bit as she pedaled, which compensated for her missing knees. It didn't take long for her skill to improve. The scratches and bruises healed quickly. The basket attached to the front of her bike allowed her to carry her books, the mail or groceries.

Ethel's challenge may have been greater than Donna's. She thought it impossible for Donna to ride the bike. She had to force herself to not say anything. She wanted to run outside and scream, "Stop it! Stop it! You're hurting yourself! You can't do it!"

Can't do it? Against all odds, Donna had learned to walk. So, with tremendous courage and restraint she watched from the living room window, tears streaming down her face as Donna took the physical beating. Her efforts had their own reward. She finally felt great joy watching Donna pedal her bike all over the countryside.

ჩ   ჩ   ჩ

May Hollingsworth, Virgil's cousin, lived a block down the street. She had never married, and had taken care of her father, Dr. Hollingsworth, the town's only physician, until he died in 1945. Her life seemed drab and lonely. The family felt obligated to visit her occasionally in her dark and cluttered parlor.

She surprised the whole family when she offered to give Donna her piano. With only two functional fingers on the left hand and legs that couldn't reach the pedals, it seemed a questionable gift.

The beautiful, black, upright Kimball was moved into the Hollingworth's tiny living room. Virgil designed an extension that would clamp onto the piano pedal with wing nuts and had it fabricated by a local ironworker. Virginia Gile, the school's music teacher, started giving Donna lessons.

Miss Gile, a dedicated teacher, taught her students to identify each of the various instruments in the orchestra. They could pick out the violins, the horns, the woodwinds and the percussion instruments with ease. They listened to the great composers, Beethoven, Bach, Mozart. She was also the focus of some rather

14

juicy gossip. In the early 1940s, female teachers were not allowed to marry. However, she had fallen in love with Charlie, the county extension agent, and they were secretly married. All of the students thought this highly romantic. Of course everyone speculated that she was pregnant. The word pregnant was not used, except in a whisper. Instead they said, "in a family way." If the School Board had known she was married, she would have been fired.

For fifty cents a lesson, she started teaching Donna how to play the piano. At first, the tedious scales drove the family nuts. The two fingers on the left hand had to work overtime to pick up all the notes and she missed a few notes, but no one seemed to notice. Before long the notes began to sound like real music. She could play "The Happy Farmer" from the *Thompson Piano Book Number One* with great enthusiasm. A love for music was born that enriched her whole life. By the time Donna was in high school, she had developed enough skill to accompany the various musical groups at school and church. Another pedal was made, so she could leave one at school and still have one at home.

The index and middle fingers of her left hand were grown together when Donna was born. She was almost eleven when Virgil and Ethel took Donna to the clinic at Wesley Hospital in Wichita. Saturday morning at Wesley, Dr. Bense, a highly skilled orthopedic surgeon, counseled with parents whose children had special physical problems. His tall, burly appearance was a bit scary, but his heart was pure gold. He suggested Donna's fingers should be separated surgically so they could be more functional. A surgery date was set. Donna was to stay in the hospital, a forty-five mile drive from home, for several days. Ethel was present for the surgery, but Donna was alone during the night and most of the day. She cried to go home with them the first night after the surgery. It broke their hearts. Although it was painful for them to leave Donna that evening, they remained steadfast.

The children's ward was on the fifth floor of the hospital. The atmosphere was cheerful, despite the abnormalities with which many children lived. The nurses and other workers were kind and thoughtful.

Donna had a small gold ring, which she wore on the third finger of her right hand. Washing her hand under the running water while the other one was bandaged, the ring slipped from her finger and disappeared down the drain. In tears, she ran and told a nurse what had happened. The nurse called and a maintenance man, who came quickly, removed the gooseneck pipe from the sink. There the ring lay in all its splendor.

Ethel was at the hospital on the morning Donna was to be discharged. When Dr. Bense came for his daily rounds, she asked him, "Is there anything that can help Donna's legs to work better?"

"Yes," he replied, with very little enthusiasm. "We can amputate her feet and fit her with artificial legs."

Donna's eyes popped wide open and she began shaking her head. "Amputate? You've got to be kidding! Never! How could I ride my bicycle?"

In his experience, artificial limbs were customized to fit over stumps that were missing part of a leg. Her feet would not fit in the "socket" that encased this stump. He wholeheartedly agreed with Donna's decision. He had worked with enough children to know how well they could adapt to the world they lived in. The power of the human spirit was incredible. Donna was no exception.

Separating the fingers helped somewhat, but it didn't give her two functional fingers instead of one. Perhaps if physical therapy had been used at that time, the results would have been better. But the middle finger remained useless because the muscles had atrophied, and it couldn't function. The index finger was limited, but she could type and play the piano much easier. It did, however, look better, cosmetically. And later on, she could wear gloves by removing the fifth finger of the glove and shortening the first two fingers. Alas, custom made gloves!

ଔ ଔ ଔ

Sarah, Donna's cousin, was two and a half years older than Donna. Neither had sisters, so they were close friends. Sarah and her family lived on their farm three miles South of South Haven. She was planning to be a medical technician although she knew very little about it. To Donna, this sounded like it might be fun, so she took courses in high school that would prepare her for the same career. The preparation courses included biology, chemistry and math, which didn't leave any hours open to enroll in the home economics courses all the other girls in her class were taking. Besides, home economics sounded boring and dull. The one course that claimed her attention was aeronautics.

Intrigued with aviation, she wanted to know how an airplane could fly. Most of her courses were difficult and challenging. Therefore, in her freshman year, she wanted an easy course to balance out her heavy schedule. Her best friend and classmate, Lucille, had told her that typing was a "snap" course. That sounded good.

The typing teacher, Miss Stevenson, was a bit befuddled. She was young, obese and had very little imagination. She had never had a typing student with only two fingers and a thumb on their left hand.

She finally confessed, "Donna, I don't know how to help you. You'll have to work out your own system."

Through trial and error, she discovered she could use the left thumb for the keys normally hit by the left forefinger and middle finger. This meant that the thumb would be responsible for nine keys—e,r,t,d,f,g,c,v,b. The right thumb would do all the work on the spacebar. It took a lot of practice, but this technique worked very well and Donna gained dexterity in her fingers. The large Royal typewriter with Donna typing at the keyboard could spin out 50 words a minute with reasonable accuracy. Miss Stevenson happily gave her a "B" in typing. The typing course turned out to be more valuable than any of her other high school classes.

The county's telephone office had three operators, one for

each eight-hour shift, but they needed a part-time relief operator. Donna, only a junior in high school could only work nights and weekends, but that seemed to work for the other operators, so despite her age, they hired her.

The phone area had approximately 300 customers. Each had a number, such as "42" or "57F15." The number of each customer was displayed on a large switchboard, with a hole below the number and a small metal piece that dropped down, indicating an in-coming call on that line. A row of twenty or more plugs fit into the holes and stretched in front of this big board, arranged in pairs. When the metal dropped down, a plug was inserted into the hole, a key opened the line and the operator said, "Number please." Then the second plug was inserted in the number requested. Most callers didn't know the phone number, so they asked for "Ted Jones" or "Andy Turner." With only three hundred numbers, it didn't take Donna long to memorize who had which numbers. Three long-distance lines connected the South Haven area to the outer world. The job was fun and it was an interesting way to get to know everyone in the calling area. Besides, it paid forty cents an hour.

Donna had a reason for wanting to earn money. She had spotted a beautiful new portable Smith-Corona typewriter for $92 at the Wellington office supply store. She would be entering college soon, and a typewriter would be necessary. Virgil and Ethel didn't offer to pay for it. Her usual attitude of "I'll do it myself" took over and she did just that. It required several hundred hours at the telephone office to get the cash together. But once purchased, she treated the typewriter gently and with great respect.

Chapter 4

We are not inferior or superior, we are different.

Donna knew boys who were her friends. There was Bud, Johnny, Dean and Jackie, but she didn't have any "boyfriends." The only time she had been kissed was at a party where everyone was playing "spin the bottle." Like most girls, she dreamed of a prince who would carry her to his castle where they would live "happily ever after." She knew she was not Cinderella, but maybe somewhere there would be a glass slipper that would fit her tiny foot.

In high school she had one date, sort of. Joe was overweight, effeminate, and not very well liked. Donna knew he had asked seventeen other girls to the combined Junior/Senior prom. They had all refused him. She was the eighteenth. Regardless of his faults, at least he was persistent in the face of rejection.

"Donna, would you go to the prom with me?"

"Of course I will," Donna replied. "Thank you for asking me." She felt sorry for him, but a date with Joe was better than no date at all.

Ethel made her a floor length evening gown. Joe presented her with a corsage. Virgil loaned them the family car. They gallantly arrived at the high school gym where the dance was taking place. Of course, she couldn't dance. Her head barely reached his waist. The miserable evening ended early with a quick kiss planted on her cheek.

When her girlfriends, Lucille, Carol and Merry talked about

their favorite subject—boys—Donna knew she was missing an exciting and special part of life, but there seemed to be nothing she could do about it. She tried to be a good sport and pretend that it didn't matter, but deep inside, it did. In order to survive this painful time, she turned her attention to other activities. She joined Campfire Girls. She read hundreds of books such as *Little Women* and *Gone with the Wind*. Family entertainment centered on playing cards and games such as cribbage, pitch and Monopoly.

She participated in these games with great enthusiasm. She diligently studied chemistry, physics, aeronautics and zoology. While her friends were going to movies and parties with their dates, Donna learned to enjoy being alone which proved to be a valuable asset throughout her life.

The effort and energy applied to her studies had their own reward. Although there were only eighteen students in her class, she graduated valedictorian. The caps and gowns for graduation were rented. Ethel couldn't cut one off at the bottom to fit Donna, so she hemmed it up. The hem measured a foot and a half, but it worked. In fact, Donna looked quite beautiful in her white cap and gown as she delivered her valedictorian address to a proud audience of family and friends.

Donna was drawn to anything that moved. First it was roller skates, then a tricycle and bicycle and later trains, cars and airplanes. Her mother called her "Donna Go." Her mother and father had given her a round-trip bus ticket to California as a graduation present. It was a seven-week trip, stopping along the way to visit relatives. She boarded the Trailways bus on that June day in 1950 in South Haven just as dawn was breaking. She was carrying only two small suitcases. Her clothes were small, so it didn't take much luggage to keep her ahead of doing laundry. She loved to travel and if possible, managed to get a seat in the front. She spent the first night with friends in Lamar, Colorado. The trip continued to Denver, Ogden, Salt Lake City, San Francisco and then Los Angeles. She found everyone friendly and interesting; the countryside was beautiful and enchanting.

Her aunt and uncle, Glenn and Reba met her at the bus station in Los Angeles and filled her next six weeks with adventure. Glenn and Reba were masters at showing their guests a good time. They sailed to Catalina, bet money on the horses at the racetrack and applauded Mary Martin in *South Pacific*. Another aunt and uncle, Ermal and Lloyd lived in Ojai. Lloyd and Donna spent hours playing cards. She went on a trip to Sequa National Park and had many picnics on the beach at Santa Barbara with all her caring family. All too soon, it was time to go home.

The trip home was not as pleasant. For supper one evening, she ate a hamburger at the bus station in Phoenix. It must have been tainted. A couple hours out of Phoenix, Donna asked the bus driver if he'd stop; she needed to throw up. He did and she did. In about thirty minutes, she asked if he could stop for a rest room. Diarrhea had been added to the vomiting. He did and she did.

By now it was the middle of the night. Someone in the back of the bus handed her a towel and washcloth. The bus driver did whatever Donna asked him to do. At the bus stop in Albuquerque, Donna phoned her mother and told her she was sick. Ethel said she would meet her bus in Oklahoma City.

Ethel had no idea how sick Donna was so she made a bed for her in the back seat of the car for the two-hour drive back to South Haven. It was a long night for both of them. At daybreak the bus pulled into Oklahoma City. Ethel was relieved to find Donna feeling much better. It would be a long, long time before a bus ride would hold any charm for Donna.

Donna spent the rest of the summer getting ready to go to Kansas University.

The classic question adults ask children is: "What do you want to be when you grow up?"

Donna's answer was always the same. "I want to be a medical technician."

Her cousin, Sarah, had planted this suggestion several years before and it seemed an impressive profession. No one else knew very much about that profession so they didn't take her seriously. Ethel suggested she take an accounting or clerical course at the junior college in Arkansas City, twenty miles East of South Haven.

Others assumed that she'd continue studying music or piano. The telephone company had offered her a full-time position as a telephone operator. All of the above sounded rather dull and boring. Besides, her brother, Jack, had gone to the University of Kansas. Jack was her hero. The application to KU was soon in the mail.

Ethel bought towels, washcloths, socks and underwear then dutifully stitched labels bearing the name of Donna June Hollingsworth on the edge of each one. They did the best they could with shoes. They had to be laced up the front to offer support and sturdy enough to withstand the twisting of her right foot when she walked. And there would be a lot of walking to do on the sprawling Lawrence campus. Slacks were easy to make and were matched with blouses and sweaters. Everything she would need was packed into two new Samsonite suitcases.

Virgil had her sign a signature card at the bank. She could write checks anytime on his account. Her parents had carefully prepared her to face each of life's challenges fearlessly. There was no resistance or apprehension to leaving home. Going off to college was just the next natural step.

Virgil and Ethel didn't share her confidence, but they didn't let Donna know about their anxiety. Besides, it was possible she'd be able to do it. It was just like learning to ride the bicycle, she'd have to discover for herself what she could or could not do. Her parents knew that it would be physically, emotionally and mentally exhausting, but they never suggested this to Donna. They'd let her go her way, free of any of their preconceived opinions that might influence her.

Chapter 5

We are in charge of what we put our attention on.

Virgil, Ethel and Donna packed the car on September 10, 1950 and headed for Lawrence, Kansas, 250 miles from South Haven.

The University campus stretched for a mile atop a large hill. The view in every direction was breathtaking. Templin Hall, Donna's dorm, sat a block off campus. In the early 1900's it was a very large, fancy, three-story Victorian home. Later it was remodeled to accommodate 35 young college women. The dining room, kitchen, parlor, library and housemother's quarters were on the main floor. An elegant staircase wound its way to the second floor with twelve rooms and only one bathroom. Each room had a desk and chair for each student.

Two to four girls shared each room. The back stairway led to the sleeping porch on the third floor with bunk beds and no heat. Many times the windows were open in the winter and snow would dust the sleeping faces. No one complained because each girl could have as many army blankets as they wanted. The top bunks were warmer, because of the heat rising above the cold air. The showers were located in the basement. It was impossible to be self-conscious about one's body or body functions for very long. Privacy was not an option. This would be Donna's home for the next four years.

Her father carried her typewriter and suitcase to her tiny room. They lingered on the large veranda and finally said their good-byes. Donna stood on the steps watching her parents drive down the winding driveway to 14th Street. A wave of homesickness flooded her. Her tear-filled eyes followed their car until it was out of sight. Her hand was trembling as she reached up for the doorknob and opened the door. Holding on to the door, she pulled herself into the dorm and began a new life as a college freshman.

It would only be speculation to imagine what Virgil and Ethel talked about on their way back to South Haven. Surely they had anxieties about the difficulties Donna would face. But they would never let Donna know that they were anxious or worried. They had resolved to set her free years ago. This was another challenge for them, just as it was for Donna.

College was not easy. The adjustment from a small high school of 300 to a college class of over 3000 nearly pulled her under. Even though Donna was an above average student, so were the other students. The competition was incredible. A Bachelor of Arts Degree in Bacteriology was necessary for entering the School of Medical Technology at the KU Medical Center after graduation. So, the first semester she took Biology, French, English and Algebra.

Not only was she mentally challenged she was physically tested. Each class was held in a different building. The ten minutes allowed between classes were sometimes not enough to get to the next class on time. Her English class was on the second floor of Frazier Hall, while the Biology class was two blocks away in Snow Hall. With books to carry and hundreds of steps to climb, her stamina was tested daily. Her feet ached at the end of the day. Fatigue lulled her tired body to sleep in the warm autumn classrooms. In the dorm, radios, typewriters, laughter and phones ringing distracted her from her studies.

At mid-term, her grade in French was a D. She was stunned. "What's wrong with me? Maybe I don't have what it takes to learn college material. Evidently I haven't tried hard enough." Fear of failure pushed her to re-double her efforts. She ate, slept and breathed French verb conjugations. *Je suis, je ne sais pas.* She made a large chart of all the verbs. Her roommate drilled her hour after hour, until she had them memorized. She studied like she had never studied before. Her efforts paid off with a B in the course.

It was a policy of the University to give parents notice when their son or daughter received any grade lower than a C. Donna's parents received this down slip regarding her grade in French. Still, they did not interfere. It was never mentioned. They knew that Donna was doing the very best she could.

Saturday nights in the dorm were usually quiet. Most of the girls had dates or were invited to parties. Alone in the dorm one Saturday night, Donna answered the phone. Several boys were looking for dates. She told each caller that no one was available. "Well, how about you?" one asked.

"I'm not interested," she replied, although a part of her was willing to give it a try. They argued several minutes. He would not accept "No" for an answer and said he would be over in fifteen minutes to pick her up. She dressed quickly and answered the door when he arrived. "I'll go get my jacket. I'll be right back," she told him. When she returned with her jacket, he was gone. She felt a mixture of relief and hurt.

Dateless Saturday nights were nothing new. She told herself it was the best night to study because the dorm was quiet. But down deep, she wanted a date as much as any girl. However, another type of call helped her with many of those gloomy Saturday nights.

A professor called wanting a baby-sitter as soon as possible. Either they had something come up suddenly, or their regular sitter couldn't make it. He sounded desperate. Since Donna was the only one in the dorm, she told him she'd baby-sit for him. She'd wait for him in the lobby.

Dr. Nellick was a gentleman and a good sport. If he felt apprehension or concern, Donna couldn't see it in his face. He courteously opened the car door for his 3'10" baby-sitter. His two children, Robbie and Joan, were six and eight years old so all three were about the same size. This fascinated the children. They all had a wonderful time playing games or reading books. The kind professor probably got an ear full from his children concerning their baby-sitter. Not only did the children like her, he felt that she was responsible and capable. He continued to schedule her to sit with Robbie and Joan. The difficult Saturday nights had taken on a new and refreshing twist.

Sophomore year was a bit easier. The discipline of learning how to study and concentrate had rescued her from the humiliation of defeat. With her head above water, she could even go to the concerts, attend the KU football and basketball games and participate in other campus activities. College life was finally becoming a pleasure instead of a struggle to survive. She enjoyed the college scene more than the boring summers in South Haven, so she enrolled in summer school between her sophomore and junior years. She applied for a job in the University Hospital on campus and they hired her to work part time in the laboratory. She had no idea of the change that would soon come in her life.

Chapter 6

The awakened being is free to experience whatever may arise.

Ken, the graduate assistant in chemistry, asked her one-day, "Donna, have you ever thought about wearing artificial legs?"

"Of course" she told him, "but I'd have to have my feet amputated to wear them."

"Check it out," he encouraged. "There may be some new developments you don't know about."

She liked Ken a lot, so just to please him she wrote to the Mayo Clinic describing her congenital deformities. Her letter finally reached someone who could advise her. He suggested she contact the P.W. Hanicke Company in Kansas City, forty miles East of Lawrence.

Seemingly content with her life just as it was, Ken had to prod her into writing the nearby prosthetics company. "Have you written them yet?" he asked.

"No, I'm not interested in being tall."

"Donna," he urged, "write them. What have you got to lose?"

Finally, she wrote again describing her physical abnormalities. She abruptly forgot the matter, assuming her efforts would be in vain.

Until . . .the next Sunday evening someone called from downstairs. "Donna, you have some visitors waiting to see you."

Curious to know who it was, she bounced down the steps to meet Betty and Erick Hanicke. Her letter intrigued Erick, a skilled German limb maker. Before he even saw her, his creative mind had come up with a method of constructing legs for her.

Erick had learned his craft from his uncle, P.W. Hanicke. Erick and his brother Werner started their business in Kansas City many years before. Erick was around fifty-years-old, a slender man, with dark hair and gentle, intelligent eyes. Betty was younger, with a solid look that said she could deal with any challenge. They directed their business and their energy toward helping people with unusual physical problems. Donna's letter captured their attention. They were anxious to meet her.

Donna ushered them into the sitting room where they made small talk for a few minutes before plunging into the purpose for their meeting.

Finally, Erick in his thick German accent told Donna, "I have thought a lot about this. Now after seeing you, I think it will work. We won't have to amputate your feet. We can construct legs for you resembling long boots that would fit over your feet and legs. The artificial knee would operate just below the tips of your toes. Your legs would operate similar to a bilateral amputee above the knee, that is, someone who had lost both their legs just above the knee joint. The ankles would be flexible. The toes and knees would bend. I've never seen a condition like yours. I would have to design and make them by trial and error."

"However, if you're willing to work with me, I'm willing to try. I would like for you to come to our shop. We will set you up on some experimental legs, just to see if you would like to be tall."

They visited for a few more minutes before they left to go back to Kansas City. "Please keep in touch with us," he urged, "and let us know when you will be coming over."

The Hanicke's information certainly added a new slant to Donna's whole situation. But did she take the next bus to Kansas City? No. Was she excited about this new development? No.

"Why would I want to go to all the trouble and expense of wearing legs? I'm doing fine without them, especially since I've learned what it takes to pass college courses. My life is running smoothly. Why would I want to change it?" This conversation kept going around and around in her head.

During the next chemistry lab she told Ken what Erick had said.

Ken was relentless. "So, make an appointment with Erick, just for the fun of it."

His persistence made Donna wonder, "Maybe Ken would like me better if I were tall."

The summer of 1952 was a hot one. The still nights were stifling. Of course in the 1950s, nothing was air-conditioned. The little Emerson fan tried courageously to stir the heavy night air with little success. Donna spent the mornings working it the hospital lab and the afternoons in the Bacteriology lab located on the 5th floor of Snow Hall. The twenty-five Bunsen burners raised the temperature to 105 degrees. The weather forecasters predicted no relief from the heat. She was still resistant to the idea of artificial legs, but thought maybe a change in scenery would be a distraction from the heat. Donna called and told Betty that she would be at their shop Saturday morning. Betty's directions to their shop were simple – half a block south of the bus terminal on the same side of the street.

Donna called a taxi to take her to the bus terminal in Lawrence. When the bus came to a stop on the ramp in Kansas City, she hopped off and began to amble slowly south. Each shop window had something interesting as she meandered down the street. Suddenly, she stopped in her tracks, frozen. There were wooden legs, back braces, pairs of crutches and a hand that looked as if it had been recently severed from someone's body.

"What do these dismembered limbs and grotesque, cold objects have to do with me?" she asked herself. "They belong to people who are handicapped or crippled. I'm neither!"

Shocked, she had to exercise great control to keep from running back to the bus station. "I can't just leave. I have to tell Erick that I've changed my mind. That shouldn't take but a few minutes." Then she could leave this eerie world and return to the hot, steamy bacteriology lab, which at that moment sounded like paradise.

Erick's enthusiasm proved overpowering. He ignored her objections and gently lifted her onto an examining table. "Donna," he explained, "we are just experimenting. We will wrap your legs and feet in plaster of Paris. When it hardens, we will attach artificial calves and feet to the bottom of the plaster. We want to see if this will work for you."

In a few minutes the plaster was set. From a closet in the back of the shop Erick found a pair of women's shapely legs with nice ankles and stylish shoes. He attached them to the plaster. Betty had a full, brightly colored red skirt that Donna pulled over her head and buttoned at the waist. They stood her up, facing a full-length mirror.

She couldn't believe her eyes. The image in the mirror was a stranger. Smiling back from that mirror was a tall, shapely coed. The difference was unbelievable. It took a few minutes for Donna to realize that the tall, beautiful image was really her own. Not consciously, but down deep inside, she felt this would be her key to romance.

Erick watched her closely. Finally, he asked her, "Donna, do you want to be tall?"

Her voice trembling with emotion, she answered, "Yes, more than anything in the world. No matter what it takes, I want to be tall."

Betty had a camera handy and quickly took pictures of Donna standing tall.

Constructing artificial legs required the creative imagination of a skilled craftsman. Erick had that gift. He explained the process to Donna.

"First, we will cut down each side of the casts that are now on your legs. When the two pieces are put together we will have an exact form. This form is filled with plaster. When the plaster is set,

30

we take the mold away again and we have sculptured duplicates of your legs and feet. We then wrap these sculptured limbs with fiberglass cloth and coat them with resin. When dry, we take them out of the mold and cut a two-inch opening down the front of each. We drill holes along the opening on each side for laces. Your leg and foot will slide into this and lace up as if it were a long boot. Next, we will construct a temporary knee joint, which is used to determine the proper point of balance. Together, we will experiment by trial and error to find that critical point. As you practice walking between parallel bars, I will make minute, delicate adjustments. Once the balance point is determined, a simple one-bolt hinge will replace the complicated knee mechanism. The resin is then covered with leather. The lower legs, ankles and feet are attached. And off you go."

He set to work, creating legs that were not only functional and comfortable but beautiful as well.

She had not told her parents of her letter to the Mayo Clinic, the following letter to the Hanickes, or the visit with Betty and Erick. Now she could hardly wait to tell them of the decision she had made—the decision to be twenty inches taller! Also, she needed $500 for the down payment.

In her letter to them she explained what had happened to her. She enclosed the pictures Betty had taken that Saturday.

When Ethel opened the letter, the pictures fell out, one landed face up on her lap. Shocked, she cried out, "What has happened to Donna?" The artificial legs looked so real that she thought they were. Quickly, she read the letter. Then reread it. Confused, she called outside to Virgil to come in quickly. Something was happening she couldn't understand yet.

They read the letter together and stared at the pictures. During the next few hours, questions poured into their conversation. Could Donna handle this physical stress? She had adjusted far beyond their expectations. She seemed happy. She was doing well in school. She had many friends. Wouldn't it be better to leave well enough alone? With a sigh of resignation, Ethel said, "It's not our decision to make. It's Donna's."

Virgil agreed. She had their full support, along with the check.

Many patients traveled hundreds of miles to reap the benefit of Erick's genius. He could not refuse to help those in need. He adjusted his hours for their convenience. Many evenings he worked in the shop until midnight, laboring over each detail until it was perfect. Saturday and Sundays were normal workdays.

Many a Saturday morning Donna climbed on the bus to Kansas City to walk on the temporary legs for hours at a time. Finally he established the point of balance where she could stand. It was similar to standing on stilts, but without holding onto anything. This point was transferred to the permanent legs. Donna was impatient to be tall and would urge him to hurry. He reminded her that walking on two artificial legs would be difficult. To give her every advantage, his work had to be done flawlessly. The only argument they had concerned the shape of the lower leg.

"Erick, the calves are too heavy. They make me look like a mountain climber or a football player," Donna complained.

"No," he insisted, "I like strong, sturdy legs," he said in his German accent. "Erick, I want slim, shapely legs. Trim them down!" she insisted. Finally, he had Betty model her legs for them.

"Do you like Betty's legs?" she asked.

With a twinkle in his eye, he said, "Of course."

"Okay, I want legs just like hers." He measured and whittled until he came very close to the shape she wanted.

Only her three roommates and a few close friends knew of the transformation in the making. Others, seeing her leave with her bags would ask, "Where are you going?"

"Kansas City," she replied.

"Again this weekend? You must be seeing someone we don't know about," they teased. "Come on, tell us about him." But Donna was determined to keep silent until the legs were finished.

Adding twenty inches to her height toppled her whole

wardrobe. Short skirts and cut-off slacks would be useless. What was she going to wear? On the next trip to Kansas City, she and Betty went shopping at the "Tall Girls" dress shop.

"I want to try on a skirt that is thirty-two inches long," she told the saleslady, who looked down at her without understanding. Checking each skirt with a tape measure, she pulled from the rack all the skirts thirty-two inches long and carried them into the fitting room. One by one, Donna tried on each skirt. The bottoms folded in a pile around her feet. "I'll take these two. They're perfect," she said. The salesperson probably thought she was absurd, but Donna volunteered nothing.

Shoes? The small, crooked shoes would go in the trashcan. Her on-going problems with shoes had come to an end. She was determined to purchase the popular rage in 1952—black and white saddle oxfords. She could also choose the size she wanted, which was an ordinary, easy to find 7B.

Just before the Christmas holidays, Erick applied the last coat of paint and tightened the final bolts. She was uncertain about riding the bus with her new legs, so Ken borrowed a car for the trip to Kansas City. It seemed fitting he would be the first to see her tall, since he had been the spark that started this whole new adventure.

Ken was uneasy about the events he had evidently set in motion. He could see more clearly the difficult changes in lifestyle she was about to face. On the way to Kansas City, he gently asked, "Donna, are you ready for this new adventure?"

"Ready?" she replied, excitedly, "I can hardly wait!" Any fear of maneuvering on these two new, beautiful legs had never entered her mind. Her resolve to be tall was unshakable. His resolve was to support her as much as possible.

At 7:30 p.m. December 18, 1952, Ken opened the door of Hanicke's at 1009 McGee Street in Kansas City. Donna entered a dressing room and changed into her new tall clothes, a yellow pleated skirt, matching cashmere sweater and black and white saddle oxfords, and threw her short clothes in the trash basket. She heard Erick come bouncing down the hall with a leg under each arm. She slipped her own legs and feet into each new leg, laced them up then she stood up to her new height. Stunned, Ken couldn't believe his eyes. Betty excitedly took pictures. Erick grinned like a new proud papa. A papa he was to the towering 5'8" girl who had just grown 20 inches before their eyes. She felt like she was meeting the world on tiptoe.

Every movement she made had to be planned. Every step she took had to be done consciously. Using aluminum band crutches she carefully walked to the car for the hour drive to Lawrence. Ken took the crutches. She lowered herself into the car seat sideways then lifted the legs in. In one hour she would make her debut into the tall world at Templin Hall's Christmas Party.

All the lights were on in the dorm when Donna lifted herself out of the car. Ken handed her the crutches and she inched carefully along the rough sidewalk. It took intense concentration to place the strange new feet in just the right place to move forward. She struggled up the seven steps to the porch. Ken opened the door and she stepped into the room.

The noisy room instantly became quiet. Conversations ceased.

"My God!" exclaimed one Catholic girl. Her hands instinctively reached for her rosary. The legs looked so real that she, and others, assumed that a miracle had taken place.

She had not practiced enough to sit down without tipping the chair over, so there she was, standing tall. She was now eye to eye with everyone in the room. She could smile into each surprised face without having to tilt her head back or yell over the noise to carry on a conversation. She was now on a level with people's faces, not their bottoms! Of course, everyone was fascinated to hear the details of what had happened to her. She started at the beginning with her letter to the Mayo clinic nine months earlier, ending with this very exciting night. Her story riveted everyone's attention.

"But I need to go to the bathroom, and I don't know how to get down on the commode." She laughed. "For years I've been lifting myself *up* on the commode. Now, suddenly, I need to let myself *down* on the commode. Looks like I've got a lot to learn about this new tall world. I'll start by climbing those twenty steps up to the bathroom."

Slowly and carefully, lifting each ten-pound-shapely leg she moved toward the top of the stairs, just in time to make the bathroom her next learning situation.

She and her roommates, Ailie, Rosanne and Gertha, talked long into the night. "Can I do this?" Donna asked, seeking some reassurance.

"Of course you can," Gertha encouraged.

"We'll do everything we can to help you," Roseanne said.

And help her they did. Ailie carried her books to classes. Rosanne held the chairs while Donna practiced sitting down in them. Gertha helped her organize her new wardrobe. They all picked her up when she fell, physically and emotionally.

The Christmas holiday break began the next day. Not yet ready to tackle the train for the long trip home, she asked a friend from Wellington, who had a car, if there would be room for her. There was. She called home and told Virgil and Ethel a time and place to meet her. Her parents saw her tall for the first time when she climbed out of the car and stood up. They were speechless.

Her voice trembling with emotion, Ethel asked, "How's it going?"

"Fine," Donna laughed, "but this tall girl sure needs some new clothes!"

Home for the holidays to visit and to practice on her legs Donna learned to open doors by pushing or pulling, then quickly placing her crutch to hold it while stepping through. To step off a curb, she put her crutch down first, then turned sideways to place her foot by the crutch, moving the second crutch down, then finally, the second foot.

Because going to the bathroom was a real struggle, she avoided drinking liquids, especially coffee. Just to stay balanced while she pulled down her panties was the first major accomplishment. From that point on, the process would go in one of several ways. Most commodes have nothing to hold on to, therefore, it was free-fall, all the way. Both hands landing on the seat she made a quick 180° pivot, hoping her bottom would hit the seat. It didn't always, but with practice, she became skillful at this very necessary procedure even if the result was a black and blue bottom.

Practicing at Erick's shop, the various chairs had sturdy arms for support. Therefore, Donna could control her descent into the chairs. Confronted now with rocking chairs, stuffed chairs, flimsy chairs, lounge chairs, lawn chairs, padded chairs, straight chairs, crooked chairs and at times broken chairs, she sometimes decided to stand. At least her feet didn't get tired.

Her brother, Delbert and his wife, also named Donna, invited her to go to the Christmas Eve program at the church. As they walked in, the pre-program commotion suddenly stopped. Silence settled over the sanctuary. Everyone froze. These people, her friends and neighbors, had watched her grow up, watched her roller-skate, ride a tricycle and then a bicycle. Some had attended her graduation from high school. Many had offered silent prayers on her behalf. They had always loved her. Now Donna was tall. They couldn't believe their eyes.

A few days later, her Aunt Hazel remarked, "You would have thought Jesus Himself had just walked in!"

As the days passed the process of walking and living on twenty-inch stilts became easier. By the time the holiday season ended, she could do a variety of tasks and movements. Donna could climb steps, stand at the kitchen sink to wash dishes, drink from water fountains, see food in cafeterias and use pay telephones. She could work at the laboratory counters at the hospital or in chemistry lab without having to use a stool to stand on. The most valuable advantage was the ability to be at eye level with those around her. This was a totally different perspective— one of great value to her. It somehow made her feel connected, or a part of, everything that was going on. And, she had to admit appearance was important. It was more comfortable to look like everyone else. In plain words, it was embarrassing to be handicapped.

With the new skirts Ethel had sewed packed in her bag, Donna returned to the KU campus. The first day back to classes was full of challenges. The chemistry professor, Dr.Burkholtz didn't recognize her and counted her absent. Friends passed her on the sidewalk and didn't speak, not realizing who she was. When she would call out their names, they would gaze in wonder at their friend, now tall.

Hundreds of steps now challenged her. It started at breakfast, the twenty steps down to the dining room, then twenty steps up to her room, and then twenty steps down for class and seven more steps down from the porch to the sidewalk. Forty steps led from the parking lot to campus level. Bacteriology was on the fifth floor. Chemistry was on the second floor. Steps. Steps. Steps. One day she counted the steps she climbed or descended—over four hundred. Inclines were tricky. She couldn't walk straight down or her knees would buckle and she would tumble. So, she had to walk down a ramp or incline sideways.

Wind, snow, ice, gravel, mud, uneven sidewalks and a hundred other situations demanded concentration. Knowing it was dangerous to walk in the snow and ice, even for those with real legs, she would call a cab to take her to class. When she fell, and she did many times, it was impossible to get up without someone helping her. Her roommates accused her of falling only when there was a good-looking man close by to help her up. But the falls were not planned. They were humbling. This "I'll do it myself gal" was learning to accept help from others, with humor and good grace. Her independent attitude was undergoing a major overhaul.

Arriving at the train station in Lawrence to go home for spring break, she discovered that the step was too high to swing her leg onto.

"Sir, could you give me a hand?" she asked one of the boarding passengers.

"Gladly," he replied, as he lifted her gently up into the train. Kind and helpful people were always nearby, if she would simply ASK. She finally understood that her self-centeredness deprived others of offering a small act of kindness. It also cracked her thick shell of self-sufficiency.

Chapter 7

If we have something interesting to do, we will not be miserable.

Before the summer term came with its stifling heat, she decided to go to the University of Wisconsin in Madison for summer school where her brother, Jack, attended graduate school. The cool temperatures and beautiful lakes combined with picking up a few college hours sounded like a great place for a summer vacation.

While riding in the airport limousine service from the airport into Madison and the University of Wisconsin campus, she noticed an Arthur Murray's Dance Studio. Dance? Why not?

After settling in at Elizabeth Waters dormitory, she called the studio and made an appointment to talk to them. She told them she walked on a prosthetic device.

"How much do the lessons cost?" she asked.

They ignored her and continued to explain the different steps they taught.

"But, how much are the lessons?" She repeated.

"Miss Hollingsworth," the studio manager finally answered, "you want to learn to dance? We want to teach you. We won't charge for lessons here."

Of course, they were interested in teaching someone with two artificial legs to dance. She'd serve as an example and inspiration to others who believed they couldn't dance.

"Look at Donna," they could say. "If she can dance with two artificial legs, surely you can dance with two good legs."

It was a promotional opportunity they couldn't ignore.

"They want to teach me to dance?" She couldn't have been more excited. They scheduled her to take a one-hour lesson every day, six days a week for eight weeks. She had to arrange her psychology and art appreciation classes around the dance lessons. Her dancing instructor was soon moving her through the waltz, tango, swing step and rumba. She became lighter on her feet as she learned to move her legs in rhythm with balance and poise.

The University of Wisconsin had a reputation as a fun place to go for the summer. Classes seemed incidental. So, one evening, after making an appearance in class, taking a dancing lesson, sunbathing on the dormitory's top deck, she and her friends decided to go out to eat and take in a movie. Any mention of homework was forbidden. As the group walked toward the theater, there was a loud pop and Donna fell to the ground. They quickly surrounded her.

"Are you hurt," one of her friends asked anxiously.

"No," she said, laughing, because there was no pain. "But I think I've just broken my ankle." They helped her to her feet, but she couldn't stand. Yes, the artificial ankle had broken. Her friends helped her to a phone and she flipped through the yellow pages to find a brace and limb shop. She dialed the number, and even though it was after hours, someone named Bill answered.

After explaining the situation, Bill offered to assist her. Since she was helpless, she accepted. He took her to his shop and inspected the ankle. A cable that attached the ankle to the calf had broken, leaving the foot dangling. He was skilled at his trade and knew exactly how to fix the cable, then drove her back to the dorm.

While driving along, Bill asked her a question that came as a total surprise. "Will you have dinner with me tomorrow night?"

A real date with this attractive young man? What could she say but, "Of course, I'd love to."

Bill was in his late twenties and wore one artificial leg. He was personable, intelligent and considerate. He had never met anyone as remarkable as Donna. He wanted his future to include her. They enjoyed going to movies and eating out. At the end of the summer he asked, "Donna, will you marry me?"

What a dilemma! Her social life was just beginning. She wasn't ready to marry yet. But what if no one else would ever ask her? "Let's give this some time," she finally told him. They parted at the end of the summer promising to write.

She returned to the University of Kansas to start her senior year. She went to see Erick the first weekend to make sure the cable was secure.

Letters from Bill came regularly. One evening in October she received a call from him. He said, "If you're free next weekend, I want to come to see you."

She didn't have the courage to tell him he was wasting his time. She knew she didn't love Bill. She just loved having a boyfriend.

He drove 750 miles to spend a couple days in Lawrence. All she knew to do was to keep him at arm's length and be cool. She was so cool she never heard from him again. A part of her was relieved. The other part wondered if she should have been more interested in him. What if she had missed her one and only chance?

Well, it was too late to worry about that! But Bill had given her a gift—the assurance that she was desirable and attractive. The phone did not ring for her, but it didn't hurt anymore.

಑   ಑   ಑

Since she had gone to summer school, she could take fewer hours during the fall and spring semesters. However, chemistry, immunology and hematology involved many time-consuming laboratory hours. In addition she was still working in the hospital lab. Most of the time she was so tired that every time she sat down, she fell asleep. Professors frown on students sleeping in class and world-renowned hematologist, Dr. Cora Downs was no exception. Donna couldn't stay awake through her 8 a.m. lecture.

After one sleepy morning, she said, "Donna, I see you have a problem staying awake. After careful consideration, I believe you are neither physically nor mentally capable of being a technician."

Donna was shocked. Hurt and anger boiled inside her. She had adamantly clung to the goal of becoming a medical technologist, even after she found out what it entailed. She had never considered doing anything else.

"What does she mean, I can't do it? She's probably resentful because I sleep in her class. I'll show her I can do it!" Anger and determination gave Donna the energy to buckle down and focus her efforts. Dr. Downs had cleverly motivated her to do her very best when she laid it on the line. Donna earned a B in Hematology. Donna Hollingsworth's name was on the Dean's List that semester.

Her roommate, Mary Ann, invited her to go home with her to Wakeeney, Kansas for the Thanksgiving holidays. Part of their family tradition was to attend a local dance during these special days. Remembering the dancing lessons, she agreed to go with her.

One unsuspecting young lad asked Donna to dance with him. Total concentration was necessary to follow the steps, so she couldn't talk and dance at the same time. He didn't say anything, either. She didn't dare fall down or they'd both be embarrassed. She was scared. He was surprised, and both were relieved when the silent ordeal was over. He carefully led her to a seat. He wasn't interested in a second dance.

Chapter 8

Joy is watching this great Intelligence handle every situation.

About two months before graduation, Donna received a phone call from her father. She knew something was wrong when she heard his voice.

"Your mother is in the hospital in Wichita. She had surgery this morning. They removed a lump from her breast. It was malignant."

Her voice trembled with fear. "Daddy, I'll be home as soon as I can." She hung up the phone, but her hand was frozen to the receiver. "Mother has never been sick. It just can't be."

It took a few minutes before she could gather her thoughts to make arrangements to be gone, probably for a week. The teachers had to be advised of her absence and give her the next few assignments. The next morning she took a cab to the train station.

Virgil met her in Arkansas City. He explained on the way to South Haven, "Last Friday your mother was drying after a bath and felt this lump under her breast. That same day she went to Dr. Ubelaker, still South Haven's only physician, he sent her to a specialist in Wichita. Surgery was scheduled for Monday morning. Since the lymph nodes were involved, they did a radical mastectomy. She's doing fine, but she'll be in the hospital for a few days."

It's not likely cancer suddenly descended on Ethel. She had lived for years with stress and anxiety. Of the four factors necessary for optimum health—reasonable activity, adequate nutrition, a pleasant environment and a peaceful, inner feeling—her feelings had been threatened the most. She and Virgil lived in a generation where feelings were not expressed. An anxiety attack, a crying fit or angry snits were not acceptable reactions. Therefore, anger, guilt or fear were not acknowledged or dealt with. These negative emotions had taken their toll in her body. Of course, Ethel was not aware of this. She had done the very best she could with the light she had to see by. In fact, she had done an outstanding job of handling life's challenges. She now had another giant issue to deal with.

As Donna walked into her mother's hospital room their eyes met. Neither said a word. Their communication was deeper than words. Standing tall beside her there was an exchange of energy, love and understanding. The courage and support Ethel had given Donna for years, was now silently returned to her.

After Virgil and Donna arrived home, Donna took off her legs and stepped into the backyard. Her favorite tree and the limb on which she used to sit had grown taller—and so had she. She climbed up, anyway, and sat for a long time in silence. An overwhelming love seemed to fill her thoughts. "The higher you climb, the further you can see. So climb higher, little one, and you will understand more. What seems to be is only an illusion. You can see beyond appearances. This is your lesson." She never forgot these words.

Although Ethel's surgery was extensive and she was taking radiation treatments, she and Virgil made plans to attend their daughter's graduation ceremony from the University of Kansas. It would take more than a bout of cancer to keep them away from it!

The university campus sits majestically on a hill overlooking the stadium below. The graduating seniors marched, two abreast, down the winding sidewalk to the stadium where the ceremonies were held. That year there were three thousand in the line. Not knowing how fast the others would walk, Donna remained near the back of the line in case she couldn't keep up. That was a mistake.

The stadium seats filled up, row by row, with the bottom row being occupied first, which put her at the very top row of seats. It was a hot June day, and her new graduation dress was soaked by the time she was seated.

According to tradition, the graduates had to walk across the platform to receive their diploma from the Governor of Kansas. Well before her name was called she began her decent. So, down the bleacher steps she went, then up the steps to the platform.

As she approached center stage, the Governor presented her with her diploma. He leaned over and whispered in her ear, "Bless you, my dear."

She certainly needed a blessing. All she could think about was all those steps back to her seat and getting out of that hot robe. Friends told her later that the crowd of 10,000 applauded her when she walked across the platform. She hadn't heard it. She probably had too much sweat in her ears.

If it hadn't been for her parents, she would have skipped the whole ceremony. But in a way, it was not her celebration, but theirs. The ritual represented a part of the reward for their years of effort and commitment. The journey from seeming hopelessness to freedom and self-sufficiency had been achieved. It was not without trial and pain. Donna's graduation from college was a victory for everyone.

Chapter 9

We will have no problems if we don't make
anything important.

In 1954 a degree was necessary to be eligible for enrollment in the School of Medical Technology at the University of Kansas Medical Center in Kansas City. With her hard-earned sheepskin in her hand, Donna applied and was accepted for the one-year program. Since the application was sent by mail, they had no idea that she wore two artificial legs. She wasn't about to volunteer the information. She was required to carry a tray of test tubes, syringes and needles. Some of the procedures would be done at the patient's bedside. Could she do it? Time would tell. The school might not have given her the chance if they had known she was walking on twenty-inch wooden stilts.

Judy Koontz and Donna had developed a warm and congenial friendship during their junior and senior years. Judy was also bacteriology major, with Medical Technology as her goal. They studied together, laughed a lot and had a warm relationship. They also enjoyed bowling once or twice a week at the Campus Lanes. After their acceptance to KUMC, they decided to share an apartment near the Medical Center.

They found a newly furnished, redecorated, three-room basement apartment, about a mile from the Medical Center. It was a bit pricey at $75 a month, but each felt they could handle $37.50. There were four steps going down to the apartment, with a small room off to the side with a washing machine and a clothesline. The living room had new red tile flooring, high casement windows, and creamy walls. A small, well equipped, kitchen separated the living room from the bedroom and bathroom. They felt like they had just rented a room in paradise.

The KUMC gave each student $60 a month as lab interns. They felt this was quite generous, since they were actually in school, not employees. Neither Judy nor Donna wanted to ask their parents for money, so they did their very best to make ends meet on their meager stipends. Bus fare was twenty cents, each way, so they walked, Donna using her two aluminum band crutches. They discovered that pork liver at 15 cents a pound was cheaper than beef liver and tasted almost the same. Instead of buying their lunch in the cafeteria at the hospital, they carried peanut butter and jelly sandwiches. This was their first step from financial dependence to financial independence. They each wanted to see if they could make it on their own. They came close. There were two items with which they needed some help: tickets to the Kansas City Philharmonic Orchestra and season tickets to Starlight, an outdoor summer theater production. Living on the edge of poverty, they felt they deserved a little fun now and then.

An internship was easier than college because there was very little homework. All of the training was with real patients, real urine and stool specimens, and real blood samples, real blood donors.

The year's program was divided into several categories. In the blood bank, they learned to screen donors, insert huge needles in veins, and process and type the blood samples. The chemistry lab tested for chloride, potassium, oxygen, sugar and other chemicals in the blood. Tests for bacteria and other invasive organisms were carried out in the bacteriology lab. In hematology, they went to the patients' room in all parts of the large medical center to obtain blood samples for testing.

Parasitology was the least glamorous of all her classes. They spent eight hours a day crouched over a microscope looking for intestinal parasites in feces. A month in that smelly lab would challenge any student's desire to become a registered technician.

Meeting patients made the month in hematology more interesting. A tray containing syringes, needles, test tubes, glass slides and alcohol sponges was carried to each patient to collect a blood sample. Donna felt very professional in her white, starched, tailored uniform and white shoes. With her right arm, she carried the tray. With her left arm, she used one aluminum crutch. This arrangement worked fine until one fateful day.

She had just collected ten blood samples. One more to go on the pediatrics floor and she'd be done. The tray was tucked securely in the bend of her right arm. The left arm was swinging the crutch in perfect timing, when a thought went through her mind, "Don't drop the tray now, you're almost finished."

At that moment, she glanced down, but failed to see the wheel of a stretcher parked in the hallway. She tripped and sprawled, belly down, on the tile floor. Blood and broken glass splattered all over everything within a radius of 30 feet. The noise of the crash brought all the nurses on the floor running to her.

They knelt beside her and asked anxiously, "Are you hurt?"

"No," she answered, mortified at the mess she had made. "But I'm sure that's hard to believe in the middle of all this blood!"

At least 50 pairs of big, round eyes watched, fascinated, as she managed to get to her feet. She gladly accepted help in cleaning up the incredible mess and began once more to collect her assigned blood samples.

 C8   C8   C8

Collecting blood was usually done in the morning. Visitors were allowed only in the afternoon and evening, 2 to 4 and 7 to 8:30. Facing a long uncomfortable day ahead of them, most patients, scared and lonely, were eager to talk to anyone. Donna, with a genuine interest in each of them, enjoyed these visits. Mr.

Evans in room 503 had leukemia. During their daily chats she found out that he owned the Chevrolet Agency in Kansas City.

"Buying a car is the very first thing I'm going to do when I get a job," Donna informed him. "In three or four months I'll have a job. I'll come by your agency as soon as I have the money."

"May I send one of my salesmen to talk to you?" he asked.

"Not yet. I don't have any income now."

He ignored her comment. "Will you talk to one of my salesman?" he repeated.

"Okay," she conceded. "I'll talk to him. Make sure he knows he may be wasting his time, because I'm not in a position to buy a car right now."

Several evenings later, a salesman came to her apartment carrying a briefcase loaded with pictures of beautiful cars. Leafing through the pictures she spotted a 1955 red and white Del Rey Club coupe.

"That's it! That's the one I want," she shouted, hugging the picture. "But sir, I don't have any money. I don't have a credit rating. I don't even have a job!"

He seemed unconcerned about the money. He ordered the car, equipped with hand controls for $2,200. She assured him that when she got a job, she would make the $200 a month car payment. He seemed satisfied with this arrangement. He advised her she would need $180 for taxes and insurance when she came to pick it up.

"One hundred and eighty dollars? That's quite a sum on $60 a month," she thought. Then she remembered she had eight $25 war bonds in the family's safe deposit box. That would do it! She called her parents and asked if they'd get the bonds out of the box and send them to her. They didn't ask what she needed them for. She didn't explain.

Of course, the salesman was not concerned about her ability to pay for the car. The owner of the automobile agency, her friend dying of leukemia, covered for her until she could make the payments. Donna did not realize this until later, too late to thank him, not only for the car, but also for his trust in her. He would make her payments until she had an income. What incredible gifts these were to her.

The next three weeks crept by. Finally the call came from the agency. The car was ready. Her landlord drove her to the Chevrolet dealership. The salesman showed her how to use the hand controls with the left hand. The single lever was attached to the steering column and worked at a 90-degree angle, push down for braking, pull down for acceleration; seemed simple enough. She checked her pulse. One-twenty. Wow! Owning a car was a giant step toward freedom. No longer would she have to struggle onto a bus or train. No longer would she have to wait for a cab. She could drive, actually drive, anywhere she wanted to go! The entire concept was almost unbelievable to her. She felt like she might explode with joy.

However, there was one small problem. She had never driven a car, and she didn't have a driver's license.

She sat down on the seat sideways and lifted her legs in and positioned them under the steering column. She started the car and slowly and carefully eased her shiny, new Chevrolet out of the parking lot. Very cautiously she inched her way through the Kansas City traffic to the courthouse. Stepping up to the counter, she said, "I would like a driver's license, please."

"Do you want a regular license or a permit to learn to drive?" the clerk asked.

"I want a regular license," Donna replied. She filled out the proper forms and signed them. And there it was—a driver's license.

"The Highway Patrol will contact you in a couple weeks to come in for a driver's test," the clerk told her and handed her a booklet to study on driving rules and regulations.

Donna knew she could learn to drive in two weeks. Arriving home, Judy's fiancé, Roger, started teaching her the skills she would need to pass the test. All three had a hilarious time touring the streets of Kansas City.

She never heard from the Highway Patrol.

She drove the 300 miles to South Haven the first weekend she had the sporty car. Her parents did not know about it. At least, she hadn't told them. She wanted it to be a surprise. As she pulled into the driveway, Ethel stepped out on the porch, her eyes widened in amazement. She was speechless. Two nights before she had dreamed that Donna had bought a new red car!

It was October of that year before she started making her car payments. The freedom to have a car to drive was a joy beyond measure. This joy has never left her.

Chapter 10

Let life unfold.

The initial thrill of having a car to drive was replaced by the nagging question of how to pay for it. Here it was the last of May. June 30 would be the last day as a student at the Medical Center. They guaranteed a job to any graduating technician, but the salary started at $242.50 per month. She had to do better than that!

"How would you like to live in Arkansas?" Judy asked.

"In Arkansas? I've never been there. Why do you ask?"

"I saw this notice on the bulletin board. A hospital in Siloam Springs, Arkansas, is looking for a technician. The starting salary is $400 a month." Judy explained. In 1955 that kind of income would solve almost any financial crisis. Donna called the number on the notice and asked if the job was still available. It was. She left for Arkansas the next morning.

When she arrived at the Siloam Springs Memorial Hospital the receptionist directed her to the office of the administrator. Donna looked very professional in her blue silk dress, blue shoes and matching hat. "I want to apply for the job of lab and x-ray technician." Donna told her. She observed Mrs. Hudson, the administrator, flinch when she saw the aluminum crutches she was using. However, she graciously gave Donna a tour through the hospital.

When they returned to the office, Donna filled out the application and handed it back to her. She sensed that Mrs. Hudson was not convinced she could handle the job, but Donna didn't want to push. So, with a cheery "Thank you for your time," a broad smile and a warm handshake, she marched off to see the town.

While sipping lemonade in the drug store, she was surprised to see Mrs. Hudson come in looking for her. Sitting in the booth, she explained, "Donna, after you left my office, I felt uncertain and confused. I decided to have Dr. Gunter talk to you."

They returned to the hospital where Dr. C. D. Gunter, Chief of Staff, introduced himself. His main interest was orthopedics, therefore, most of the conversation centered on her congenital deformity and the artificial legs. He was fascinated. Finally, he asked, "Walk across the room for me." She did, without the crutches. "You do remarkably well on those legs, young lady," he commented.

She really wanted the job. Everyone was kind and friendly. She felt at home in this small Arkansas town. Maybe the interview with Dr. Gunter would give her a chance.

Mrs. Hudson promised to call after the next day's staff meeting at which all of the applications would be reviewed and a decision would be made.

When the call came, her heart nearly stopped. She was afraid to answer the phone and afraid not to.

Mrs. Hudson said, "Donna, we want to hire you as part of our staff. How soon can you start to work?"

Relief? Excitement? Her mind was spinning. Finally, she collected her thoughts, remembering she had four days of vacation available. "I'll be there on June 27."

Later, she learned that Dr. Gunter had said to the staff, "I don't know if Donna can handle this job or not, but I feel we have a responsibility to let her try."

Judy and Roger helped her pack the car for the move to Arkansas. All her belongings fit neatly in the trunk and back seat— the faithful typewriter, some books, a few clothes and six new tailor-made uniforms. Although she was leaving friends and familiar, comfortable surroundings, she was fearless. The beautiful

Ozark Mountains seemed to open their arms and enfold her as she drove the winding roads to Siloam Springs. She felt like the luckiest girl in the whole world. Her heart nearly burst with gratitude.

Mrs. Hudson had found a furnished apartment for her near the hospital. Virgil and Ethel drove the 240 miles from South Haven to help her unpack and move into her new apartment.

They were interested in seeing the hospital and town. After getting her things in order at her apartment, they toured the city of 3000 where Donna would live.

They were continually amazed at her self-sufficiency, not realizing the remarkable contribution they had made to her independence.

Chapter 11

Every challenge is an opportunity to grow.

Her position was supervisor of the lab and x-ray departments. The laboratory work was routine—blood counts, blood sugars, chemistries, bacteriology, urinalyses and EKGs. She had one small problem; she didn't know how to take x-rays. She put the heavy x-ray books in the darkroom and studied whenever she had a free minute. Whenever there was a request to x-ray a patient's chest, she would turn to the index in the book, and look under "chest." Then she would study the pictures to decide how to position the patient. A large chart explained how to set the control knobs on the massive machine.

"Take a deep breath. Hold it." Click. "Now you may breathe."

Legs, chest, arms, fingers, toes, knees, elbows were easy to x-ray, a form of photography. A sub-mandibular joint was a bit tricky. Patiently, Dr. Curl, the radiologist tutored her but he drove down from Joplin only one day a week. The technician who was leaving also helped her. Trial and error proved to be an excellent way to learn.

With her limited knowledge of x-ray, emergencies were terrifying. The first weekend she was on duty was the Fourth of July, 1955. She froze when she heard the ambulances go out, sirens screaming. It could be a long night since she was on-call and sure enough, in a few minutes the phone rang. Even though she was expecting it, she jumped a foot when it rang. She headed to the hospital, heart pounding. When she walked through the emergency door, one victim, apparently dead, lay on a stretcher completely covered with a blanket; another was waiting in the x-ray room. Blood transfusions were needed for still another victim. She took a deep breath. She asked the doctors what they wanted her to do first. Blood was the priority. In a pinch, the doctors could take their own x-rays. So, she started with the transfusions.

The hospital had what they called a "walking blood bank." Those in the community interested and able to give blood were typed and the information kept on file. When a patient needed a transfusion, his blood was typed and a donor was called with the same type of blood. To save time, a cross-match could be started while the donor gave the pint of blood, which took about ten minutes. Two a.m. was the ideal time to call donors. They were at home and sensed the urgency of the call. Of course, the donors were proud to give blood and felt like they had saved someone's life, and they probably had. The system worked very well, and the charge to the recipient was for the lab work and infusion only. The blood was free.

Dr. Curl, the radiologist, came every Tuesday to read the previous week's x-rays and do fluoroscopy, upper GI series and barium enemas. Part of Donna's job was to hold the barium can high so the barium would gravity feed. With the room darkened, Dr. Curl used the fluoroscope, watching as the barium entered the patient's large intestine. Then Donna helped the patient to the bathroom, hopefully before he lost his bowel-full of barium. Sometimes he didn't make it.

One elderly man they worked with was as deaf as "a doorknob." Dr. Curl nodded for Donna to switch off the lights overhead.

In the darkness, Donna screamed in the old man's ear. "We're giving you an enema. Hold it. Don't let it go."

The fluoroscope moved slowly across his abdomen. As her eyes adjusted to the darkness, she could dimly see barium covering the x-ray table like huge amoebas.

"Hold it. Hold your enema," she yelled once again in his ear. Still, she could hear the drip, drip, drip of the barium hitting the floor. When Dr. Curl finished the exam and the lights were turned on, the patient, soaked in barium was clutching the enema tube for dear life. He was simply following instructions, as he understood them. It wasn't his fault he was such a mess.

Walking without crutches or canes became her routine. She couldn't climb steps without a handrail or someone to help her, so she carried canes in the car for emergencies. Because she wore the legs so continuously, lumps occasionally developed in her groin area. Sometimes they had to be drained. Beyond that, the legs were comfortable and she was not conscious of them. They seemed to be a part of her body. Many people thought she had had polio because of the way she walked. She didn't bother to correct them. It was just too complicated to explain.

In 1957 she made several trips to Kansas City so Erick could make a second pair of legs. A new outer covering for the lower limbs had been developed that looked like real skin, right down to the toenails. The foot was designed to wear a two-inch heel, which looked very classy. With coordinated skirts and blazers, the result was striking.

The loan on the car had been paid off months before, so Donna paid for the legs herself this time.

Chapter 12

Let life unfold naturally.

Reba, a registered nurse at the hospital and Donna became good buddies. Reba had graduated from nursing school in Tulsa. When her marriage dissolved, she and her son, Danny, moved back to Siloam Springs to live with her parents. She and Donna decided to take their two weeks of vacation time in August and drive to Colorado.

They spent the first night with Virgil and Ethel in South Haven. The red and white Del Rey was ready for the trip, however, it didn't have air-conditioning. Knowing Western Kansas would be hot, they decided to leave from South Haven at sundown. Although they alternated driving and stopped every two hours for coffee, this was not quite enough to keep them awake.

At 4:00 a.m. on Friday morning, Donna was driving though Colorado Springs. A sudden jolt and loud crunch woke both of them up. In that split second of sleep, she had run off the road and the car rammed into a light pole. The police came shortly, called a wrecker to haul the damaged car to the Chevrolet dealer, and took Reba and Donna to the police station. It seemed like the place to go at that time of the morning. Donna received two tickets: one for careless driving and the other for damaging public property. The court hearing was set for Monday morning at 8:00 a.m.

Since friends in Boulder were expecting them, they climbed on a bus for the hundred-mile trip. Early Monday morning they returned by bus to Colorado Springs for the hearing. Trying to climb on the bus, Donna stumbled and fell. A young gentleman picked her up and dusted her off. They laughed, introduced themselves. He said his name was Jack, "How about a cup of coffee when you get back to Boulder?"

"I'd love it," she replied, breathlessly.

The courtroom was full that Monday morning. The police had experienced a busy weekend. When her name was finally called, the judge asked her if she was guilty or not guilty to the charge of careless driving.

"Not guilty, your honor," she replied.

"To the charge of destroying public property, how do you plead?" he asked.

"Not guilty." Out of the corner of her eye she saw the policeman who had arrested her signal to her. She had to plead guilty to that charge because the light pole was the tangible evidence of her guilt. Evidently the judge realized that this young lady in front of him was new at court proceedings. He lectured her on driving when sleepy and fined her $100 for the light pole. She was told where to pay the clerk and was then dismissed.

Golden Chevrolet, the dealership, assured her the car would be repaired in two weeks, in time for the trip back home to Arkansas.

Sure enough, her new friend, Jack, called the next evening. He was a professor at the University of Colorado with a brilliant mind, beautiful blue eyes, warm smile, ready laughter and a gentle spirit—a very attractive combination. Donna imagined herself in love, which may have meant she liked the guy and heard the mating call at the same time. Whatever it was, it caused her thoughts to turn in the direction of moving to Colorado.

The time had come to ride the bus back to Colorado Springs to pick up the car at Golden Chevrolet. It looked brand new and the insurance company paid for it all. It would not be necessary for her parents to ever know the car accident had happened. Besides, who could say that the accident was good or bad or terrible or tragic? Because of it she had met the love of her life. Maybe there are no accidents!

A few months later she applied for a job as a medical technologist at the Rocky Flats Atomic Energy Plant. The interview went well and they agreed to hire her, contingent on her security clearance. Back home, she packed her bags in anticipation. Disappointment came in the form of an apologetic letter saying they doubted her physical capacity to deal with the snow and wind in Colorado. She was crushed.

"What do they mean, I can't do it? Of course I can do it."

But their decision was final.

Determined to move to Colorado, she applied for a job at the Fitzsimmons Veterans Administration Hospital. This job required a Civil Service rating, which she applied for and was given a GS-7 rating. As soon as a job opened up, she would receive their call. She was ready to move from Siloam Springs and the Memorial Hospital. She gave the apartment owner thirty days notice.

But life had other plans for her.

Chapter 13

If we are finding fault, we are looking through a misconception.

Neal Lancaster was a charmer. His troubled past had not destroyed him but had strengthened and matured him. Neal and his twin brother, Allen, were born April 10, 1911. Allen died when he was nine months old of spinal meningitis. Neal, the youngest of four other children, was clearly his mother's favorite child.

Drinking was not uncommon, nor was it banned at home. But like an invisible cancer, it insidiously took control of Neal's life. Not understanding what was happening to him, his jobs, his families, his relationships, he ended up in jail in Carlsbad, New Mexico. He was convicted of beating up a four-year old boy. The judge advised him to never return to Artesia, New Mexico. Neal had no recollection of the crime. He was in an alcoholic blackout at the time. He could not believe that he had committed this despicable act. His sense of guilt and self-loathing were overwhelming.

Six months before his arrest, he had cut a clipping out of an "El Paso Times" newspaper. It said: "If you want to drink, that's your business. If you want to stop drinking, that's our business." It was signed: "Alcoholics Anonymous."

The penal authorities found this clipping in his billfold. After a few days, they asked Neal if he would like to contact AA. At this point, his despair was so great that he was certain he was losing his mind. He would have agreed to anything. So, in 1947, a call was made to an AA member, who came to the jail to see Neal. He was allowed to leave the prison to go to AA meetings. This was the beginning of a lifetime of service in the program of Alcoholic Anonymous. Eventually, the judge who had run him out of Artesia invited him back to Artesia to start an AA group.

In 1950 he returned to Siloam Springs, married, and on January 28, 1952, his beautiful daughter, Lisa, was born.

The marriage couldn't survive. The divorce was final in 1956.

Neal had found some answers to living in the Twelve-Step program of Alcoholics Anonymous. He had finally realized that he was powerless over alcohol and that his life was unmanageable. He had come to believe in a Power that could restore him to sanity. He asked for serenity to accept the things he could not change, courage to change the things he could and wisdom to know the difference. His happy, loving, carefree nature was set free to love his life and the people in it. He found a purpose for living that had a new dimension and a new meaning. He was at peace with himself and the world he lived in. He was enjoying living alone and had no intention of getting involved with another woman.

Then he met Donna.

ଔ ଔ ଔ

Neal lived across the street from Donna's first apartment in Siloam Springs. He noticed her parents helping her move in on that hot June day in 1955. At the time he thought, she'd be an interesting person to know. It would be over two years before he would meet her.

Mike and Lorraine Moss were Donna's close friends. They encouraged her when the days at work were too long and comforted her when she had been at the hospital all night. They made her feel a part of their family. Their neighbor, Odessa Holland, had a room she wanted to rent, four blocks from the hospital. Of course, in a town of 3000, nearly everything is four blocks from the hospital. Mike felt Donna and Odessa would be perfect for each other and arranged for them to meet.

In her sixties, Odessa had raised five children with wisdom and loving discipline. She was tall and slender, with a wrinkled face reflecting years of responsibility and hard work. Yet her voice, smile and eyes reflected inner joy. Her second husband of ten years had died recently. Her ingrained nurturing nature drew her to Donna.

They came to an agreement on the room rental of twenty-five dollars a month, which included all the bills, and Donna could use the kitchen. The arrangement was perfect for both of them.

She knew Donna wanted to move to Colorado. She listened patiently to all the conversation on how wonderful he was and how excited she was to be moving. Odessa helped her when the job at Rocky Flats fell through, softening the blow of that disappointment.

"We don't know the future," she would gently say. "Everything has a way of working out to our advantage. The past is dead. The future is an unwritten page. Let's cherish right now, for that is all we have."

Donna and Lorraine were sitting at the Mosses' kitchen table one October afternoon drinking a glass of iced tea when Mike and Neal came in the door. They had been on the golf course all afternoon. This was the first time Donna had met Neal face-to-face. He was slender, medium height, balding, with happy eyes and a contagious laugh. Everything he said was funny. She found his sense of humor awfully appealing and thought him a fun guy.

When she got back to her room, the phone was ringing. It was Neal.

"I understand you have a girl working for you in the hospital lab by the name of Sally, who has a drug problem. Could you meet me for coffee and talk about what we can do for Sally?" he asked.

"Of course," Donna replied. They made arrangements to meet the following evening at Neal's apartment.

She told Odessa she was having coffee with Neal Lancaster

the next evening. Odessa had known Neal and his family for many years.

Her only comment was, "If you don't want to fall in love with him, you better not see him."

Donna did not cancel the date.

Over a cup of coffee at the kitchen table Neal told Donna the story of his alcoholism. He left nothing out—the drinking, the three marriages, the many lost jobs, the two attempts at suicide, the beating of the boy… jail. He laid it all out, or so she thought, without justification or self-condemnation. That was just the way it was. He did not plan to become an alcoholic. It was something that happened to him and he was powerless to stop it. His guilt and remorse were so painful he drank over and over to deaden the pain. He was trapped in a bottle of self-destruction, with seemingly no way out.

He had just passed a milestone, over four years of sobriety. But still there were no guarantees that he would not drink again. His sobriety was contingent on the maintenance of his spiritual fitness, one day at a time. His participation in the AA program gave him spiritual food, based on the necessity of working with others with similar problems.

Neal had used Sally as an excuse to call Donna. During their three-hour conversation, he never even mentioned Sally. Later on, armed with a brief introduction to AA from Neal, Donna did encourage Sally to attend meetings but her mind was so befuddled with drugs that she couldn't grasp the program. She disappeared and no one ever knew what happened to her.

But that first visit over coffee ended with an invitation to Donna to go to an open AA meeting.

The next evening, Neal picked Donna up at Odessa's. When she started to open the car door, he gently slapped her hand.

"I was taught that a man opens a car door for a woman," he said gently. Another opportunity for this I'll do it myself gal to learn to accept other's gifts graciously.

The AA meeting was fascinating. The people there, alcoholics and their spouses were warm and friendly. The talks about their destructive past, what happened to change their lives, and what was going on now, were open and honest. A lot of their escapades were hilarious in retrospect. To be able to laugh at themselves instead of condemning their behavior was a great freedom.

Lisa, Neal's six-year old daughter, was a dear. She was tall for her age, with intelligent eyes, dark hair, and the wisdom of sixty years instead of six. She and Donna liked each other right off. Aware Lisa might be jealous of anyone capturing her father's attention, Donna made sure that she was included in conversations and activities.

By the end of thirty days, seeing each other every night for supper, then to a movie or an AA meeting, Neal wanted Donna to meet his family.

Kathryn, Neal's sister, invited them to dinner. She and her husband, Bodie, lived in Gravette, 25 miles north of Siloam Springs. Donna realized that she was going for family approval, which made her nervous.

After dinner, while helping Kathryn with the dishes, Donna commented on what a fine person Neal was.

Kathryn turned abruptly to Donna and said, "You don't have to tell me how great he is. I've known him longer than you have."

For a moment, Donna was shaken. Then she realized Kathryn was teasing. Kathryn wouldn't tease anyone she didn't like.

"What about the exciting move to Colorado and that heartthrob she had wanted to be near?" She had almost forgotten what the move to Colorado was all about. The grass was getting greener each day in Arkansas.

During the Christmas holidays, they visited Neal's other sister, Frances, and her husband in Tulsa.

While driving down Riverside Drive on the way to their house, Neal asked, "Donna, will you marry me?"

They had teased and laughed about getting married. In fact,

she had longed to hear those words. Now, here they were. The big question was did she really want to live with Neal day in and day out? Did she really love him? How would he feel about her if she said no? It was fun to dream about marriage, but was she ready to accept the challenge and reality of it? Minutes passed in silence. She didn't have any answers to the questions she was asking herself. Then the nesting impulse took over and she said, "Yes."

Both Kathryn and Frances knew of Neal's stormy past. They knew he was in AA and his life was now smoother. They only wanted him to be happy. Donna seemed wise enough to do her share to make the relationship work. And with three marriages behind him, he had, hopefully, accumulated some information and experience that would be helpful. Frances wished them well.

One situation had to be faced before the wedding plans could go any further. Neal had not seen Donna without her artificial legs. She was used to bouncing back and forth between 3'10" and 5'8," but she was now planning to have a housemate, and this roommate had never seen her short. Donna worried he wouldn't like her short or like her different body. What if her body repulsed him? She wondered if he could accept her naked. One afternoon she dressed in her little clothes and invited him over.

She went limp with relief when he held her and said tenderly, "Donna, your legs make no difference to me. It's you that I love."

They talked about having children. As far as she knew, she had all the necessary equipment to conceive and carry a child. Although her periods had not begun until late in her teens, they had been regular. A caesarian section would have been necessary instead of natural childbirth because of the shape of her pelvis and lower back. They decided not to have children because of their age difference and the possibility of problems at childbirth. Neal volunteered to have a vasectomy, which made the decision final. Besides, they had Lisa.

Lisa was beginning to suspect that her beloved daddy was planning to marry Donna. One evening after their favorite meal of hamburgers and French fries, she asked Neal to sit in the big chair, with Donna on one arm, while she sat on the other.

She then laid a big Bible on his lap and asked, "Daddy, do you really love Donna?"

"Yes," he replied.

"Would you be happy married to Donna?" she continued.

"Yes," Neal said.

"If you marry Donna, do you promise, on the Bible, you will never fuss with her?"

"Yes," he promised.

Lisa then asked Donna the same three questions, getting the same answers.

Then she proudly announced, her bright eyes smiling, "I think it is just all right for you two to get married."

Donna had answered the questions Lisa asked and gave the answers she was expected to give. But this marriage situation was uncharted territory. Did she really love Neal? He was considerate, patient, fun and seemed reasonably responsible. She liked him. But love? She really didn't know what that meant.

She suspected there was more to it than having fun in bed. The question about happiness, she had no clue what happiness was. Happiness was more than having everything going one's way or being comfortable all the time. That would certainly not be realistic. Excitement was not the same as happiness. Excitement was too nebulous and short-lived. Happiness, peace, serenity, joy—words that were ill defined, yet seemed worthy of attaining. Happy with Neal? That, too, was an unknown. And the last question about not fussing. Neal seemed easy going. But, twenty-four hours a day, seven days a week? She couldn't even say that her own emotions would never erupt into anger, resentment, sulkiness or irritability. That would be asking a bit too much. The only thing she could do was to do the best she could do. She felt like she was jumping out of an airplane and the parachute was not guaranteed to open.

Virgil and Ethel knew nothing of the whirlwind courtship between their daughter and Neal. In fact, they knew very little about her social life. As far as they knew she had never had a date. Marriage was never considered. So, when Donna called and said, "Neal and I are getting married. Is it all right for us to visit you this weekend?"

They were stunned. The silence on the other end of the phone was interminable. Finally Ethel managed to say, "Of course. We'll be expecting you."

"Donna married?" It took some time for this to register. "A son-in-law?" This was a whole new area of speculation and suspense. What kind of a person was Neal? Knowing Donna as they did, they had better like him, because her decisions were usually set in concrete. To raise any objections would be futile.

To their surprise and delight, Neal was charming and likable. He had a remarkable ability to put other people at ease, so everyone had a good time. He was even willing to learn to play pitch, a game the family had played for years. Politely, Neal asked Virgil if he could marry their daughter.

Virgil had only one comment: "Be good to Donna." Ethel had one question for Donna, "If something happened to Lisa's mother, would you be willing to raise her as your own?"

"Yes," Donna replied, "Lisa is everything I could want in a child of my own."

The day before the wedding, Neal and Donna went to the bank to put their accounts together. When the teller showed them their accounts, Donna had several hundred dollars. She looked at Neal's account in disbelief. He had $1.37. She was surprised. He was relieved that he was not overdrawn. One thing was certain. She was not marrying him for his money! At least he had a job at the lumberyard.

The date was set—February 23, 1958 at 4:00 p.m. in the Methodist chapel. Roy, Neal's long-time friend, was best man. Reba, Donna's friend who had vacationed in Colorado with her, was maid of honor. The guest list was simple. Virgil, Ethel, Delbert and his wife, Donna, came from South Haven. Neal's brother, John, and his wife, Polly from Ponca City, Kathryn and Bodie drove down from Gravette, Frances and Doc arrived from Tulsa, and of course, Odessa. All of Neal's relatives were relieved he had found someone as delightful and responsible as Donna. Donna's family was somewhat cautious because of Neal's turbulent past.

Neal's previous marriages had ended in disaster, yet here he was at the altar again. Doubts had been crowding his mind as to whether he was capable of making a marriage work. He loved Donna so much that he was terrified he would fail once more. It was too late to back out now. He earnestly prayed he would not hurt her. His hand was shaking when he took Donna's hand to say the marriage vows they had memorized. In a few moments it was over as the minister said, "I pronounce you husband and wife."

Odessa had prepared a reception at her home for the wedding party. Cake was cut and served along with non-alcoholic punch. Pictures were taken. Everyone put their concerns behind them and celebrated this union. Everyone wished Neal and Donna a happy life.

Chapter 14

*We would feel fantastic and enjoy ourselves
if we dropped all expectations.*

Neal had been living in a three-room furnished apartment above a garage, which rented for $25 a month. Donna moved in, made new curtains and painted the cabinets. While she was unpacking and re-arranging the closets, she noticed all of Neal's ties were tied and the short ends cut off. How strange. When she asked him about it, he explained that he could not tie his tie. So he had someone else tie it for him. He would then loosen it just enough to slip it over his head. The next time he wore the tie, all he had to do was to slip it back over his head and pull it around his collar. The longer he followed this routine, the longer the short end became, so he had to cut off the short end to keep it from showing below the long end. Simple solution to a knotty problem! They both laughed hysterically.

Neal helped Donna with everything except the cooking. If their day at work had been busy and long, they ate out. They both enjoyed having a clean, uncluttered environment. They placed dirty socks in the clothes hamper and shoes neatly in the bottom of the closet. They made their bed before they left for work.

Donna was on call five nights a week and every other weekend. If it was especially difficult for Donna to get dressed and go to the hospital in the middle of the night, Neal would go with her. During a phone call, Neal's brother, John, asked how they were getting along.

Neal said, "We're getting along great! I let Donna have her way in the things that matter. She lets me have my way in the things that don't matter!"

There were some tough lessons to learn, however, such as accepting another person, just as he is. Neal was rarely out of sorts, but when he was, Donna wanted to fix him.

"What's wrong?" she asked, assuming it was something she had done.

"Nothing's wrong," he grumbled.

She had to learn to let him be responsible for his own mood, without her interference. Likewise, Neal had to let Donna work out her own conflicts. It required practice to stand back and let the other person be free. Fortunately they each had Twelve-Step programs to help them learn these new skills

When they had an invitation to go out with friends, Donna became tense.

Neal's reaction to plans of any kind was irritability, and his response was, "No, I don't want to go."

After a time, Donna learned to say, "That's okay, you do whatever you want to do. I believe I'll go."

Reluctantly, sometimes he decided to go. He usually had more fun than anyone else. Occasionally, he stayed home and Donna stayed home with him. Gradually, they learned to give each other the freedom to do what each wanted to do, and not feel guilty. Donna played bridge every Monday night. Neal never objected. They tried never to place unreasonable demands on each other. Most of the time, they succeeded.

The summer after they were married, Neal received a scholarship to the Yale Summer School on Alcohol Studies. This would mean being away from home for over a month. The hospital gave Donna the month of July off and the lumberyard did the same for Neal. It would take three days to drive to Schenectady, New York, where Jack, and his wife, Nancy lived. Donna would stay with them while Neal was in school at Yale University in New Haven, Connecticut.

They squeezed everything they'd need for the long trip into the car. Excited about the trip and unable to sleep, they dressed, turned off the lights, picked up a thermos of coffee, locked the door and left at 3:00 a.m.

Chapter 15

Let circumstances be.

House plans were beginning to cover the kitchen table. This was the first sign of house heat. The apartment was cheap and comfortable, but the time had come for a real home. They mentioned this desire one evening during dinner with Leon and Cleo, who lived at Lake Frances, six miles south of Siloam Springs. They knew of a real bargain, just down the road from them.

"This house and seven lots near the lake can be bought for $1,500. It's a steal," Leon said. "Let's go look at it."

The single lane, rutty road was a bit of a chore to maneuver, but once down the hill, this cabin, nestled in pine trees had possibilities. There was a leaky roof, knotty pine walls, screened in front porch, falling down back porch and a fireplace that didn't work. The plumbing was clearly marginal and the septic system needed some fixing. After assessing the work required, the initial price of $1,500 was the least of the expenses.

Leon knew the owner and arranged a meeting to discuss the sale of this cottage in the pines.

When they were discussing the sale price Neal, less enthusiastic than Donna, said, "There's no way we'll pay that price; $1,350 is our top dollar."

When the seller looked at Donna, she had big tears in her eyes, he knew the sale was in the bag. Sold—at $1,500. The house was on land that could possibly be divided into seven lots in all with uncertain boundaries. There was also a view of Lake Frances if one had the courage to stand on a ten-foot ladder in the back yard or climb to the top of one of the pine trees.

The work began. The dark wood floors were sanded and refinished. They turned out to be a beautiful white pine. A light colored tan stucco was applied to the outside with matching brown trim. The new roofing matched the stucco and trim. They started over in the small kitchen with a built-in oven, food bar, new sink and cabinets, and new refrigerator. The back porch was torn off and replaced with a 20 by 20 sunroom, with nothing but windows on three sides. They poured a 14 by 20 patio in the back yard and added a carport.

They hired someone to do most of the work. However, Donna wanted to paint the trim on the screens, all forty of them. Her plan was to spend her two days off working on this project. Once the task had begun and momentum mounted, she decided to go as far as she could before she had to clean the paintbrushes. By the time Neal came rumbling down the rocky road at 6:00 p.m., she was done with all of them. Barely able to lift her arms and covered in brown paint, she proudly showed Neal the stack of neatly painted screens.

There were several drawbacks to this paradise in the country. In the winter, the road was almost impassable. Also, Donna was on call at the hospital, which meant a six-mile trip to the hospital that often took over ten minutes. An outside bell was installed to the telephone so Donna could hear the phone ring when she was in the yard. Since they lived in the country, their telephone was on a line with four other parties, which was not always convenient.

Donna was cooking spaghetti and cheese for dinner when the hospital called. Someone had fallen and they needed an x-ray. The spaghetti was already cooking when she left and she forgot to tell Neal when to take it off the stove. Ten minutes later he tried to call the hospital to ask her, but someone else was using the telephone party line.

74

Finally, in desperation, he interrupted the conversation and asked, "Can one of you ladies tell me how long to cook spaghetti?"

"Cook spaghetti?" Neal explained what he needed and they laughingly told him.

They enjoyed eating their evening meals on the patio watching the wrens, cardinals, chipmunks and other fascinating wildlife. Occasionally, they would see a copperhead or a stinging scorpion.

Then there was Molly, their two-year old female boxer. She could not stay in the house while they were at work, so they built her a doghouse that matched the cottage. She didn't like it. Donna even crawled into the house with a tasty morsel of steak and tried to get Molly to crawl in with her. Molly wouldn't budge…until… One very cold morning when the temperature was about zero degrees. As they drove out of the driveway, they saw Molly's eyes peeking out from behind the carpet they had hung over the door of her cozy nest.

Molly also insisted on sleeping on the couch, which they did not approve of in their tidy home. They finally set a mousetrap. When she leaped onto the couch, the trap sprung. She was so frightened that the couch never interested her again.

She was an intelligent, delightful, playful companion except when she passed gas, which nearly drove them out of the house.

CB   CB   CB

Neal decided to get involved in politics. He joked it seemed easier than working for a living. He filed to run for the position of City Clerk and Treasurer, a very courageous undertaking for him. Even though he had been born and raised in Siloam Springs, the whole town knew of his alcoholism and his rocky past. Some people knew that he had not had a drink for ten years. Yet, it was questionable whether he would have enough votes to win the election. A politician at heart, he won the election easily though. However, a city ordinance required he live within the city limits.

Reluctantly, they listed their country home and property for sale. Even though it was on a dead end road that was nearly inaccessible in the wintertime, once found, it was a prize. Potential buyers just could not see it through their eyes. They sold it at a stinging loss.

Fortunately they both had good incomes, which totaled $800 a month. In the early sixties, their banker knew this was more than adequate and loaned them $16,500 for a new home.

They built a three-bedroom brick home in the south part of town. This project took the edge off of their sadness in leaving the country. They adapted quickly to central heat and air conditioning, paved streets, coaxial TV, wall-to-wall carpeting, city sewer system, garbage disposal, washing machine and clothes dryer. Since Donna seldom wore her legs at home, they had the carpenter build a pullout shelf in one of the lower cabinets, which served as a workbench.

Their home was warm and friendly, a reflection of the host and hostess. Neal and Donna had many friends who, with very little urging, came for the weekend. These guests now had their own bathroom in which the lavatory would drain and the stool would flush.

Life was very good.

Donna with her first bike. At 12 she taught herself
how to ride it despite the doubts of others.

Donna's high school graduation picture – 1950.

Donna at Sequioa National Park in 1950.

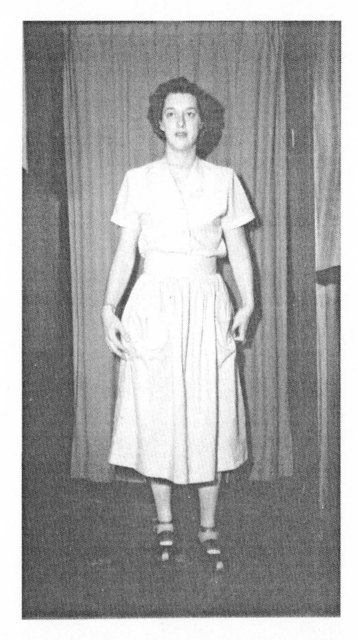

Donna with her "new legs" in 1952. She stood at 5'8" tall.
"I felt a little unsteady here. The dark piece at the ankle joint works
like a normal one. The foot bends at the toes. I felt ten feet tall."

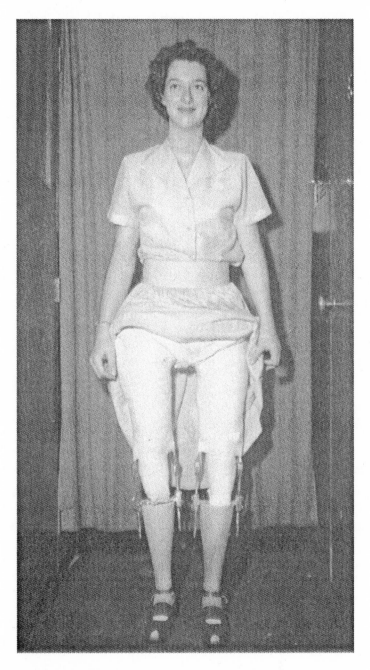

Beneath the dress, Donna shows the artificial legs that gave her "normal" height.

Donna at the University of Kansas in the Spring of 1953.

Donna with her new car in 1955, Kansas City, Missouri.
She loved that car and the independence it gave her.

Donna and husband Neal at the airport in
Wellington, Kansas in the mid 1970s.

Donna and an experimental, home-built aircraft at the Arlington, Texas airport in 1993. The plane was built by Leon Davis and is the Davis II, serial number 1. It only weighed 600 pounds.

Donna has always loved music and it has been an important part of her life. Here she enjoys playing the piano in Ojai, California in 1981.

Chapter 16

Inner conflict is dangerous and fatal.

Nearly every month they drove to South Haven to see Ethel and Virgil. Ethel was not well. She had gone to the doctor with pain in her back, shoulders and arms. He was treating her for arthritis. Because her pain continued, the doctor finally sent her to a bone specialist for a check-up and x-rays.

The next Sunday morning, Virgil called and said, "Your mother is in the hospital for treatments. The cancer has spread into the lungs, bones and God only knows where else. The treatments she is taking will not cure her, only decrease the pain."

Donna felt like a knife had just been plunged into her stomach. She knew her mother was fatally ill.

She and Neal went to church that morning. Donna quietly cried throughout the service. By the time the church service was over, a calm acceptance had replaced most of the hurt.

Wanting the situation to be different would not make her mother well. "What is, is what is," Donna reasoned. She would be as cheerful and helpful as possible and make these last few months easier for everyone. Each weekend, Neal and Donna drove to South Haven to be with Virgil and Ethel.

As long as she was able, Ethel baked a chocolate pie each Saturday and had it waiting for them. At times, Ethel would bake the crust, then rest; make the pudding, then rest; then finish with the meringue. She was totally free of self-pity and never complained. She was consistently cheerful and optimistic. Since she was always ready to play cards or games, they had many wonderful evenings.

Then the time came when she couldn't make it to the bathroom or to the table to eat. Virgil had his hands full with laundry, meals and caring for her. He would never have asked Donna to come home to help him, but was genuinely pleased when she offered and came to stay with him until it was over, until Ethel passed away.

It was not easy to watch Ethel's body slowly waste away from lack of food, but she couldn't eat. If she could have, she would have. But she could not. Ethel knew, as did the whole town, that she was dying. It was no secret. However, like sex and religion, death and dying were never discussed. No one, not even Donna, or Virgil, Jack or Delbert had the courage to talk to her about her fatal condition. They could however, take care of her and maintain a pleasant atmosphere. Hundreds of friends came, bringing food or flowers, showing their love for her. The physical acts of caring were obvious from everyone. The sharing of this very personal act of dying was missing. Unfortunately, that was just the way it was. The concept of hospice care had not yet reached rural Kansas.

Neal came over from Siloam Springs every weekend. He loved Ethel, as she did him. Donna had been her greatest concern for thirty years. She was peaceful with the knowledge that Neal would take care of her.

She died as she had lived, with courage and acceptance.

Chapter 17

If our attention is not on this moment,
our awareness is fragmented.

Eleven years had past since Donna had started to work at the Siloam Springs Memorial Hospital. Although she had worked her way up and earned a salary that allowed Neal and her to have many comforts, she was at a point where she didn't want to go to work. She watched the clock and counted the minutes until quitting time. She felt put upon when a child broke their arm and needed an x-ray just as she was leaving to go home. She pulled the covers over her head and groaned when the phone rang at night for a call to the hospital. The most satisfying part of the week was her time off. The enthusiasm and creativity she once had were gone. These were compelling signals it was time for a change. So, she quit her job.

She didn't quit before she had another one, however. The medical clinic adjacent to the hospital needed a lab and x-ray technician. The salary was better, the hours more regular, and the work easier. She applied for the position and got it. There were, though, some drawbacks. The winter of 1968 was bitterly cold. The clinic didn't have central heat and air-conditioning. They used an open space heater. The wind had swung to the north during the night. When Donna arrived at work, the office was freezing cold. Shivering, she turned on the heater and stood with her back to it, trying to stay warm. In a few minutes she smelled something strange. She then realized she had been too close to the fire and the backs of her legs were burning. The hose on them had melted and the paint was blistered. Luckily she only needed sandpaper and paint instead of an emergency room because something was about to happen to her and Neal that would dramatically change their lives. The benefits of this new job, more time, more energy, more money, would help to make their new adventure possible. Before beginning her new job, Donna and Neal decided to take a vacation.

After a week's vacation in the beautiful Wyoming Mountains, they headed home. The highway seemed to stretch endlessly before them. It was going to be a long day of driving. "I wish we could fly," Donna sighed, wearily.

"Why don't we?" Neal replied.

Something happened inside of Donna. At that moment, an excitement began to build into a realization that flying was not impossible – even for her. There had to be some unseen force that allowed an aircraft to fly. That's why she took aeronautics in high school so she could understand this incredible phenomenon. She learned it took the wind longer to go over the top of the wing than it did to flow under the wing. This created a vacuum on top of the wing that pulled the plane up. She had never forgotten her first plane ride in a Piper Cub.

When Delbert returned from the service, he started taking flying lessons. Donna was always ready to go with him to the airport, just to watch the planes take off and land. One day, his instructor offered to take her for a ride. She had never forgotten this magical experience. The remaining miles on that hot July afternoon seemed to just whiz by as she began to accept the possibility that maybe, just maybe, she could learn to fly.

Their close friends, Roy and Erma, influenced their decision to learn to fly. Roy, Erma and Neal had grown up together in Siloam Springs. When Roy returned from California in the early sixties, he was a shaking, sick and miserable alcoholic. Neal became his AA sponsor. They traveled to AA meetings nearly every night. Roy never drank again. Erma was co-owner with her brother of Allen

Canning Company east of Siloam Springs. Roy and Erma fell in love and married. The canning company needed a plane and pilot. Roy had always wanted to fly, and filled this position with great passion. Just as Donna would do later, flying consumed his every thought and word. Donna's attention hung on his every word, fascinated with his flying stories.

Erma's legs were paralyzed, the result of a back injury when she was a young girl. Roy had designed some hand controls for the brakes and rudders, and after having them custom made, installed them in their Cessna Skyline so Erma could learn to fly. Roy knew similar hand controlled brakes and rudders could be made that would work for Donna. So, the first step, they decided, was to buy an airplane. Roy suggested they call Ed Reeve, a skilled flight instructor at the Siloam Springs Airport (now called Smith Field). Ed knew of a Skyhawk in excellent condition for sale at the airport. He felt it was worth the asking price of $6000.

The next morning, Neal and Donna went again to their friendly, generous banker and borrowed money to buy a plane, which neither of them could fly. Their credit rating was outstanding; he didn't even ask them if they could fly the plane before he loaned them the money to buy it.

"Ed, now that we have this airplane, I need to learn to fly it. Can you teach me to fly?" she asked hopefully.

"Can you drive a car?" he asked.

"Of course I can," she answered.

"Then you can learn to fly," he said.

"We bought an airplane," Donna told her coworkers at the Medical Center.

"You what?" they asked in a tone that indicated madness.

"You don't know how to fly," they teased.

"Of course we don't," Neal laughed. "We can't even start it!"

"You guys are crazy," they concluded, shaking their heads.

Flying, as she discovered later, was not quite as simple as driving a car, nor was Ed as confident as he had led her to believe.

He was however, wise enough to avoid any suggestions that might dampen her enthusiasm. He sensed the belief in her ability and the intensity of her desire would overcome any and all obstacles. He was right.

Roy worked with them to design the hand controls, and an ironworker in town made them. A metal plate was clamped on each of the foot pedals. From this plate, a rod extended upward. There were short handles on the top of each rod, which rested on the seat between her legs. With her hands, she could use each of the rods, independently or together, pushing forward for brakes or pressing downward for rudder control. But first, she had to learn the function of the rudder.

July 24, 1971, 5:00 a.m. The airport beacon was still making its knife-like sweeps through the countryside as she drove down the narrow lane to the hangar. She was meeting Ed for her first flying lesson. She had to learn how to pre-flight the 1960 Cessna Skyhawk, to insure safety of flight. They looked at the air pressure in the tires while walking up to the plane. It would be embarrassing and dangerous to land a plane that had a flat tire.

The gas cap was unscrewed and a long stick was dipped inside the tank, then pulled out to confirm the tank was full. The cowling was opened and the oil checked. The engine had to have oil pressure to operate, so the dipstick was securely locked into place. Gasoline can't have even a few drops of water in it, so a sump button drained away any water. The prop was felt for nicks by running a hand along the leading edges. The rudders, ailerons and control wheel were checked for freedom of movement. *And, oh yes, check for bird nests in every small opening.*

Ed guided her though the pre-flight checklist, then watched as she maneuvered the rudders to turn the plane right or left. They taxied to the end of the runway. The plane was equipped with dual controls, so Ed could take over, if necessary. They checked the sky for any other planes in the pattern, then gradually pushed in the power. The plane moved slowly at first then gained momentum. In a few moments the tiny craft lifted from the runway and they were airborne. To her amazement, flying was more fun than she ever dreamed it would be. The view was breathtaking. They leveled off at 3000 feet and practiced simple maneuvers, such as going up, down, right, or left. Time was up quickly for the first lesson. Ed smoothly squeaked the plane back onto the runway.

Donna had no illusions about becoming a famous pilot. She just knew that flying was something special, which justified spending all the money, time and energy she could muster. The stirring within had something to do with an innate sense of freedom.

She was born as a free spirit, which somehow seemed trapped in a body, a job and a society. Flying seemed to diminish these limitations. It was like non-identifying from the world and just observing it, rather than being emotionally involved in all its problems. This produced exhilaration beyond measure. This airborne world of order, harmony and peace seemed much more real than the illusionary world of heartache and misery.

Everything in flying is a learned reflex action with one exception...instinct. Instinct keeps the pilot from flying the plane into the ground. Starting the engine was a pattern that had to be repeated over and over until the sequence was established and automatic. Attention was required to remember that the wingspan would easily bump into buildings or other planes and the propeller was a lethal weapon. Throughout the lessons, Ed gave her information he had acquired from his 20,000 hours of flying experience.

"I'm teaching you a sequence of actions which will result in safe flying. Follow it implicitly. Your life may depend on it."

During some lessons, Ed would say, "Isn't it a beautiful day?" This would challenge her concentration to hold the wings level, airspeed constant, altitude steady, heading right on course, talk on the radio – all of these activities at the same time. The lessons stretched her mind and ability. Eventually, after hundreds of flying hours, she could carry on a conversation, manicure her nails and fly the plane all at the same time.

When she started the flying lessons, the other pilots at the airport had been skeptical and aloof. To fly with hand controlled brakes and rudders would be dangerous and impossible. They thought her flying was just a brief fling. She'd soon realize how difficult it was to maneuver the craft without using her own legs and feet. Although she always flew with her artificial legs on, they were useless to operate the foot controls. Faced with these difficulties, they expected her to lose interest and quit. With apprehension, they watched as she spent hours and hours to practice this skill, which required hard work and focused attention. In a few weeks they understood, as pilots, her fierce determination to learn to fly. They eagerly gave her support and shared their experiences. These pilot friends had never seen a student with hand-controlled brakes and rudders fly a plane. Realizing it would require a great deal more skill and perseverance to fly a hand-controlled aircraft, they watched her practice landings with great concern for her safety. They really wanted her to make it.

On August 23, 1971, Neal said he was going to the airport with her for her lesson. She was suspicious. She had less than 20 hours, but the time had come for her to solo. This meant managing the aircraft as the only person on board. As pilot in command of an aircraft three takeoffs and landings had to be made to qualify to fly the plane alone.

Sure enough, after a couple of swings around the flight pattern in the cool, calm morning air, Ed said to stop the plane near the taxiway. He crawled out of the cockpit, looked up at her and said, "It's all yours. Good luck!"

There she was, alone, with the instructions to make 3 takeoffs and landings. Her heart was beating so fast she couldn't catch her breath.

Then, very carefully, she taxied to the end of the runway, radioed she was departing runway 36, released the brakes and pushed in the power. The plane began to move down the runway, gaining momentum each second. When the speed was sufficient to support flight, she gently pulled back on the wheel. The aircraft lifted gracefully from the runway. Within seconds she and her tiny craft were airborne. Would she ever get it back on the ground without crashing it? Probably not. She realized she had to focus her attention on the techniques Ed had taught her. She reduced the power setting to 80 RPM, held the altitude at 2000 feet and entered the downwind pattern, slowly losing altitude, then entered crosswind, and turned on final approach. She cut the power, raised the nose of the plane very gently and carefully. The plane settled over the runway.

She heard the squeak of the tires. "Whew! Two more landings to go," she said. Drenched in sweat, adrenaline pumping, and a bit of confidence emerging, the next two were over without killing herself and/or wrecking the plane.

She taxied up to the ramp, opened the door of the plane to climb out and was surrounded by a huge crowd. The other pilots hugged her and cut off her shirttail to hang on the office wall, as is the custom for those who have just soloed. Neal hugged her. Ed was relieved.

To anyone who has never soloed, the feeling is inexplicable. The feelings of accomplishment and joy were overwhelming. Her face seemed welded into a permanent grin. At the end of the day, her face ached because she couldn't keep from smiling.

Studying for the required written exam to obtain a license was a breeze. Each night she would rush through dinner, then reach for the books while Neal did the dishes. Her mind was riveted to principles of flight, mechanics of an aircraft, FAA regulations, navigation and weather. By Thanksgiving she had passed the written exam. The desire to learn everything in these books was compulsive. In fact, flying was compulsive. She ate it, breathed it, walked it, talked it, dreamed about it and bored the hell out of anybody who would stand still for a minute and listen to her babble on about how wonderful it was. Their eyes would glaze over and they would smile patiently.

Neal solidly supported her flying. He never questioned the money or the time spent in this venture. He praised her when the landings were good and comforted her when they weren't. When she despaired of ever learning all the complicated procedures and wanted to sell the plane and forget the whole thing, he paid no attention. He had taken four lessons from Ed and decided it was too tough for him. He could understand how overwhelming it could be. But he could also understand how much she loved the sky and would not let her quit if he could help it

The FAA required certification of the hand controls. Blueprints were sent to the engineering department in Fort Worth. The FAA sent their engineer to Siloam Springs to inspect them and issue a document number 337. All of this seemed tedious and time-consuming.

Donna spent the next few months flying solo, along with a few more lessons on instrument and night flying and cross-country flying. Before long she was ready for the big one—the exam for the pilot's license. All the requirements were met and she was ready for the flight exam. Since she had a medical waiver on her medical certificate, a medical flight examiner at the GADO office in Little Rock had to give her the flight test. This was scary business. Siloam Springs had an uncontrolled airport, requiring very little radio communication. However, Adams Field at Little Rock had approach control, control tower, ground control and radio communications that had to be followed. The Skyhawk had an old Mark V radio, which could either communicate or navigate (VOR), but could not do both at the same time. The solo flight to Little Rock was fun and she miraculously found Adams Field. Since she did not have her license yet, she could not carry passengers.

Neal and Ed flew in another plane to Little Rock. They checked into a motel and Donna went to bed early, anticipating the following demanding day. Sleep wouldn't come. The more she told herself how important it was to get a good night's rest, the more awake she became. Her eyelids seemed frozen wide open. Dawn finally came.

The flight examiner omitted nothing. For the first two hours he gave her problems on weights and balances, cross-country planning and other questions. Finally he said, "Let's go fly."

They started across the ramp to the plane. Donna stumbled on a rock and fell flat on her face. She felt like a fool. The examiner helped her up and happily climbed into the plane with her anyway.

He watched intently as she made each landing, each take-off, and each of the many emergency procedures. The two hours and twenty minutes seemed like days. He finally suggested they return to Adams Field.

"Whew! It's finally over," she thought. She set the course for Little Rock and radioed approach control. In a few minutes she contacted the control tower and was cleared to land on runway 35. The final approach was fine, but she leveled off four feet above the runway. The examiner had to take over the controls and land the plane. Donna was heartsick and wanted to cry. She knew she had failed the exam.

The examiner climbed out and said, "I'll meet you upstairs in a few minutes."

Neal walked over to the plane and asked, "How did it go?"

With a huge lump in her throat and on the verge of tears she said, "I didn't pass."

"Is he just leaving you here on the ramp?" Neal asked incredulously.

"No, he wants to talk to me," she answered half-heartedly.

As they walked toward the office, she began to think of several prospects that might be interested in buying a Skyhawk, priced for quick sale.

Sitting across from the examiner's desk, he told her some things on which she needed to practice. Then he said, "Donna, you're a safe pilot. We're giving you a license."

Several seconds passed before she realized what he had said. "You're just kidding me," she finally said.

No, he wasn't kidding. At that very moment she became a licensed aircraft pilot. Relief, joy, amazement, gratitude, disbelief. The hard-earned ticket was really hers. The moment was exquisitely beautiful!

Neal could fly back to Siloam Springs with her now that she had the license. Twenty miles south of the airport she radioed, "N7724X, 20 miles south inbound for landing. And by the way, I have a passenger." The guys at the airport knew she had gone to Little Rock for the check-ride. They also knew that if she had a passenger she had passed. They cheered her home.

Chapter 18

We can all handle "what is."

They had flown to Hot Springs on Friday afternoon the first week in August 1973 for the annual AA Convention. As soon as the last meeting was over, they took a cab to the Hot Springs Airport. The temperature was a sweltering 100 degrees and the still air was loaded with an oppressive haze. The weather briefing indicated scattered clouds at 3000 feet and four miles visibility, a typical August afternoon. Climbing to 8500 feet after take-off, the temperature gradually decreased about four degrees for every 1000 feet. They leveled off in the cool 68-degree temperature and sat back to enjoy the puffy white cumulous clouds surrounding them.

Suddenly the engine sputtered, coughed, then sputtered again. "What's going on?" Neal gasped.

Donna quickly pulled the carburetor heat (to melt ice that accumulates and stops the flow of fuel to the engine) and followed the emergency checklist. Her hands were trembling and her heart was beating so fast she couldn't breathe. She radioed the Hot Springs control tower and told them she had an emergency. "It looks like the engine is failing!" Neal was pumping the throttle, but the altimeter was quickly unwinding—8400, 8300, 8200. . . . Pumping the throttle seemed to be the only thing keeping the engine running at all.

"N7724X, what is your position from Little Rock?" the Hot Springs tower asked.

"24X is 274 degrees off Little Rock," she replied.

"24X, you are 20 miles northwest of Hot Springs," they advised.

The altimeter now read 5000 feet. That's above sea level. The mountains under them rose 2800 feet above sea level. They had 2200 feet of space below them. Descending at 500 feet per minute at an airspeed of 80 miles an hour, 20 miles would take 15 minutes. But they only had four minutes and 24 seconds before.... She also knew that beneath the scattered clouds lay a blanket of haze, and then trees, trees and more trees. No roads. No highways. No pastures. Nothing but trees.

"Hot Springs tower, 24X will never make it."

The tower cleared all other air traffic to another frequency, alerted the rescue units, and stayed with 24X. From the trembling in her voice, they knew she was scared. Meanwhile, Neal's pumping the throttle seemed to be leveling the engine out. Power was returning spasmodically. The prop was turning faster. Just before they slipped into the clouds, the engine started running smoothly. They kept the tower informed of their progress. The tower told them to climb back to 7500 feet, if possible.

"24X, the sky is mostly overcast, but there's a hole in the clouds just northwest of the airport. Hold 7500 feet, if you can, until you have the airport in sight."

Seconds seemed like hours. They had just experienced a potentially fatal situation. They were scared, but was it fear of dying? Probably. They were so busy doing the right things that eminent death was not a conscious thought.

Their eyes searched for a glimpse of the airport. Then they saw it.

"There it is!" they yelled. "24X has the field in sight!" she radioed.

"24X is cleared to land," the tower answered. "And I bet that's the prettiest sight you've seen all day! Give us a call when you get on the ground."

They spiraled down from 7500 feet, swung left to enter final approach, landed and taxied to the ramp.

"What do you think happened?" the controller asked.

"There are three possibilities," Donna replied. "The first, and most likely the cause of our problem was carburetor ice, especially on such a hot humid day. The second possibility could have been debris in the fuel line, and thirdly, Cessna 172's are susceptible to vapor locking at altitudes above 5000 feet."

The mechanics checked the plane carefully. Everything was in perfect order. They could find nothing wrong. After a sandwich from the airport restaurant, they climbed back into the plane. The rest of the trip back home was comparatively dull.

Chapter 19

If we don't have to be safe, we have no fear.

Just for the fun of it, Donna took a Real Estate course by correspondence from the University of Arkansas. The material was terribly dull. However, once she started she felt duty bound to finish it. After she passed the final, she thought that while the material was still fresh in her mind, it would be a good time to take the state broker's exam. Since the exam was only given in Little Rock, this gave her a good excuse to fly. She didn't tell them she had never darkened the door of a Real Estate office. She passed the test and they gave her a broker's license anyway.

Their next-door neighbor, Walter Gray, owned the best agency in town. When he learned Donna was taking the course, he told her, "I have a desk and office waiting for you when you're ready to start selling Real Estate."

It would be a bit of a gamble, though. The cost of keeping an airplane was significant. The salary at the Medical Center along with Neal's salary at City Hall was paying the bills. Would she be able to sell enough to bring in some income? She had never sold a piece of property in her whole life. She might not like selling any more than she liked being a technician. "Oh, well, I'll never know unless I try it," she thought. So, she quit the boring and dreary job at the Medical Center.

Of course she didn't know how to sell. She hung around the office, attended the sales meetings and started acquainting herself with the listings. She joined the sales force on the tours to see new listings. For the first time in 18 years she was working with physically healthy people.... A healthy change for her.

Weeks went by without a sale, or even a client to show property. Then one July morning in 1972 some people came in and she was the only sales person available. She told them they were her first clients, which helped to relieve some of her anxiety. Fumbling through the qualifying process they were very patient with her. Finally, they all left her office to look at some listings that fit their needs. Unbelievably, they liked the first place she showed them and wanted to buy it. She was so stunned she could hardly write up the sales contract. A couple of times she didn't know how to fill in some of the blanks. Walter helped her. In several weeks she received her first commission check. "Hmmm," she thought, "this might turn out to be a better deal than I thought." She started taking her work more seriously.

All of the sales people rotated the days they were scheduled to be "up." This meant they were responsible for walk-in clients. This was Donna's day. A couple from Wichita, Joe and Mary, wanted to look at 90 wooded acres on the Illinois River. They could only look at part of it by car; not all of the terrain was passable. On the way back to town Donna asked, "Would you like to see that 90 acres from the air?"

What could they say? They were captive in her car! "Of course," they said.

They stopped at the airport and Donna pulled the plane from the hangar.

She caught Joe cutting his eyes at her, silently asking, amazed, "Is she the pilot? What have we gotten ourselves into?"

"Let's go," she called.

They were good sports and climbed into the plane. The winding Arkansas River and the towering pines looked beautiful from the air. They circled and circled until the property lines were clearly defined. They landed back at the airport and taxied up to the ramp. She heard Joe mumble, "I don't believe this."

Joe and Mary bought the property.

Walter sent her to Tulsa one fall day to pick up a client arriving from California. Tulsa International Airport had a parking place for small planes located close to the arriving gates. She taxied to this area, parked the plane and walked to the gate to wait for the client. When he came, she introduced herself and they walked to the exit. "How far is it to Siloam Springs?" he asked.

"About 90 miles," she answered. "We can be there in thirty minutes."

He looked at her strangely. She directed him to the plane. It was then he realized what was going on.

"Do you mind flying in a small plane?" she asked, unlocking the right door for him. What could he say?

The trip could not have been more beautiful. The fall leaves were red, orange, yellow, maroon and sprinkled with a thousand hues of combined colors. The tall green pines provided a background for this spectacular display. They flew low, soaking in the rich colors. He hardly noticed the pilot wore artificial legs and used hand controls to fly the plane.

Her co-workers affectionately called her their corporate pilot. She flew their clients over farms and ranches. Sometimes she flew to distant places for closings on Real Estate purchases. She loved it!

Chapter 20

Depression is another word for self-pity.

As long as Donna could do things to keep distracted, she could ignore the growing sense of hopelessness and despair inside of her. She had fun at the Real Estate office or when she was flying. But home alone with Neal was becoming increasingly difficult. The feeling of being trapped lay just under the surface. She covered it with a smile and a positive attitude so that outwardly everything looked fine. They went to AA meetings together. Entertained many friends. Flew to conventions and meetings all over the country. At many of these meetings both she and Neal were speakers. It would seem that they adored each other and life could not be better.

But she couldn't stand for him to touch her.

At night before going to sleep, she felt a hopelessness. The effort to put on the happy face and pretend everything was lovely when it was not drained her energy. Fatigue was her constant companion. There was uneasiness just under the surface, a feeling of something not quite right.

"Surely there must be something wrong with me," she concluded.

She was reading all the self-help books she could lay her hands on. She had gone to the Christian Church for years, hoping to find some answers. Neal was a member of the First Christian Church and she had given it her best shot. They went to Church on Sunday morning and night and prayer meeting on Wednesday. She just couldn't choke down what they were teaching. Then she and Neal became involved in the Unity Church. In fact, they had flown to the Unity Village near Kansas City several times on Sunday morning to services. The Unity teachings seemed easier for her to digest and understand.

Finally, in 1975 she turned to a counselor. She told him how she felt about Neal.

He said, "Donna, feeling the way you do, you have two choices. You can wait around until he dies, or you can get a divorce. As your friend and counselor, I'm telling you to leave the marriage. Leave the marriage!"

That was not what she wanted to hear. That had not been an option. It had just never occurred to her to get a divorce. "I can't do that," she sobbed. "I don't have a reason to leave."

"As strongly as you feel, you don't need a reason," he replied.

Desperate, she said, "I want you to tell me how to change my attitude so I can stay in the marriage."

He had no answer.

The next few years became progressively more difficult. Neal's retirement only accentuated the problem since he was always home. He seemed to love her, which made it more difficult. He never put her down or made her feel stupid. He was supportive in everything she did, complimented her on every meal, liked everything she bought and admired everything she wore.

Why would she feel all this aversion to him? She was married to a charming, kind, thoughtful husband, but she didn't want to live with him. She tried everything to change how she felt. She read theology and philosophy books. Surely the great writers and religious teachers had some clues about how to have peace and joy and serenity, regardless of the circumstances.

Belief in God seemed to be a running thread in all the books. The Twelve-Step program suggested, "letting go and letting God" or "turning your life and will over to the care of God." She tried all that over and over. At times it would work. But ultimately she would end up hopeless and depressed. Was there any system or creed or information that would work consistently?

"Maybe I just need to grow up," she thought. "Am I missing something that would allow me to live in peace, regardless of the circumstances and people around me? Or is life just a blend of heartache and happiness and all I have to do is grit my teeth, take the bitter with the better, and maybe I can make it. Make it to what?' What was it that kept her from being happy? Right Now!"

She had all the creature comforts. What was she whining about? The Twelve-Step program of AA seemed the closest to working. The results were visible in those who worked the program. Their lives reflected an inner change of some sort that couldn't be understood or denied.

The questions were endless and tiresome. There had to be more to life than making a living, having a relationship, paying off debts, building a dream house, or buying new clothes or a new car. "Is that all there is?" she wondered. The last desperate words each night before sleep came were: "God help me."

In 1979 a dear friend invited her to come to Whitney, Texas for the weekend. The flight to Texas was a routine one. She had made many trips to Whitney to attend seminars held in a special chapel. The round building was called the Chapel of Light. The lower floor was used for office space, a lounge, kitchen and restrooms. The upper level provided a meeting place, a sanctuary, surrounded by thirteen large windows. Each window reflected a different hue of rainbow colors. People came from all parts of the country to enjoy the peace that always seemed to be present.

The Chapel was the result of a dream Marce White, a long-time friend, had in 1971. It was not something she wanted to build, but the impressions were so strong that she shared the dream with a few close friends. They supported her and the project was soon started. To raise money for the construction, monthly seminars were offered that included teaching spiritual truths, which avoided all denominational creeds and doctrines. Since Donna was searching, searching, searching, she was pulled to Whitney many times.

Friends met her at the airport and took her to their home for the weekend. After one Saturday morning session, Marce invited her to lunch. Sitting on her deck overlooking Lake Whitney, Marce said, "We're looking for a coordinator for the Chapel."

Without thinking, Donna said, "Where do I apply?"

They talked about what the duties and responsibilities of a coordinator would be. Marce explained she would be running the book store, setting up weekend seminars, arranging Sunday services, inviting speakers, keeping track of the money, making financial reports, writing and sending out a monthly newsletter and working with the 12-member Board of Trustees.

Donna wanted the job. Maybe some of her uneasiness would be resolved in this spiritual atmosphere. She was willing to take some drastic steps to find some peace.

When she got home to Siloam Springs, she told Neal about the conversations with Marce. Neal was ready to go to Whitney. He had retired from the city office three years earlier and living on the lake seemed like a wonderful idea. In fact, he was convinced they needed to move to Whitney and would not listen to Donna when she wavered about moving there. Donna wasn't sure about coordinating a Chapel. In her state of mind it wasn't likely she could handle it. However, the Board of Trustees thought she could do it and hired her.

They leased their home, called a moving company, packed the cars and headed for Texas. They couldn't fly the plane to Texas. The large, steel hangar door had slipped from its track, skinning the leading edge of the wing. The plane was in the shop for repairs.

One of the Chapel friends let them live in their rent home until they decided to build or buy a house. Half of their furniture was put in storage because the house was so small. The wonderful conveniences of a garbage disposal, central heat and air, storage space and two bathrooms were things of the past. Adapting to these changes took its toll. There was no room to be alone. Neal was always there. On her day off, she wanted to run away from home.

"What in the hell is wrong with me?" she cried.

She listened intently to the Chapel speakers, read hundreds of books, meditated, and earnestly sought the answer to her feelings of being trapped. Depression hovered over her like a dark cloud. There seemed to be no answer.

On Friday, October 10, 1979 Donna came home to find Neal sitting on the couch, struggling for each breath. "What's wrong?" she cried out, sensing that something terrible had happened. "I had a sharp pain in my chest this morning and I've had trouble breathing ever since," he gasped.

"Do you want to go to the doctor?" she asked.

"No," he replied. "If I'm not better by morning, I'll go then." He was not better. He was worse. Unable to breathe lying down, he had sat up all night—without sleep.

The doctor believed Neal's emphysema was causing the shortness of breath. He gave him some medicine and sent him home. The medicine brought no relief. Neal had another sleepless, breathless, miserable night. Donna knew he was going to die if he didn't get some medical help. On Sunday, she called the doctor and he said to take Neal to the hospital. The x-rays revealed a collapsed lung. They rushed him to the emergency room and inserted a tube through his ribs to re-inflate his lung. He was in the hospital for six days.

Donna felt scared and very guilty. She had not been the easiest person to live with lately. She regretted being so touchy and irritable with him. What if he had died? She would have carried a load of guilt around for a long time. After he came home to recover, she tried harder to let him know she loved him. But did she love him? Something was terribly wrong and it had to be something wrong with her.

Neal seemed to be doing well, so Donna and three friends, Elwin, Marce and Sherry, traveled to Austin to attend a lecture by a speaker they wanted to hear. They were all part of the Chapel group, and were always looking for new speakers they could invite to the Chapel for a seminar or weekend workshop.

Before leaving the motel the next morning, Donna suddenly stumbled backward and fell on her left hip. She tried to stand up, but couldn't. She took her legs off and tried to stand and walk. She couldn't. The pain was so severe that she couldn't move. Her friends filled the tub with hot water and helped her into it, hoping that soaking would relieve the pain. It didn't help. She had fallen hundreds of times and had never hurt herself.

"Surely the pain will go away shortly," she sobbed.

If she sat real still, there was no pain. So she put her legs back on very carefully. The bellboy carried her to the car and they started the 140-mile trip back to Whitney. Everyone was so hungry that by the time they were on the road, they decided to stop at the Stagecoach Inn in Salado. Donna thought by this time the pain would be gone. Wrong. The moment she tried to stand, the pain was incredible.

The only way she could get into the restaurant was on her hands and wooden knees. Donna crawled to the entrance, up the steps and through the door, feeling ridiculous and silly. She had to go to the bathroom immediately, so she crawled to the bathroom and pulled herself onto the toilet. "What a relief!" she sighed. But the dining room seemed five miles away. She didn't need to worry. Her creative friends brought a high chair on rollers to the restroom, helped her onto it and wheeled her to a table.

The dinner was outstanding. When they were ready to leave, two men carried her to the car. Elwin insisted they stop by Scott and White Clinic in Temple to see about Donna's injury. The x-rays showed no broken bones. Of course, she couldn't break a hip. She didn't have any. However, the muscles, ligaments and tendons were injured and would take time to heal.

During this healing time, with or without legs, she was nearly helpless. She didn't like it. Everywhere she went, even at the Chapel, she had to ask someone to carry her. This crazy accident reminded her, again, how loving and helpful people want to be when given a chance. She found her old aluminum armband crutches and started using them again. Little by little she recovered. Just in time to attend her Daddy's funeral.

Chapter 21

It is easy to lie to ourselves.

Two years after Donna's mother's death, Virgil had re-married. Everyone loved Gladys, his new wife. Gladys, Ethel and Virgil had gone to high school together and had been friends for years. Virgil had retired from the gasoline business in 1954. He had bought 230 acres of land south of town. Part of the land was pasture and he bought cattle to put on it. Seventy acres were in wheat. He and Gladys loved to fish on the three ponds.

They had many good times, went dancing and played cards. On Christmas day, 1975, she died suddenly from a heart attack. Without Gladys, the loneliness and pain were more than Virgil could bear. Alcohol was the only thing that would ease the pain and let him sleep. He felt useless. At 75, he thought he was too old to find a purpose for living. Depression was his constant companion. Donna would fly to South Haven to see him at least once a month.

"What do I have to live for?" he would ask her.

She had no answers for him. She was asking herself the same questions. There had to be more to life than money, cars, dream-homes and sex. But what?

"Where is the joy of living? What is it that makes life worthwhile?" The questions played over and over in Donna's mind.

All she could do for Virgil was to thank him for the life he and Ethel had given her. They had allowed her to have the freedom to manage her own life without interference, suggestions or judgment. What an incredible gift they had given her!

On April 2, 1980 Delbert called Donna at the Chapel. Their Daddy was dead. They would never know if his death was an accident or intentional. He had gone to the farm that morning to feed the cattle. Delbert saw him around noon and noticed he had been drinking. The next morning they couldn't find him. They pulled the garage door up. He was in the car. The death certificate said, "Carbon monoxide poisoning."

Donna was really okay with his death. She knew her daddy had done the best he could do with what light he had to see by. He could not have done it any differently. If he could have done it differently, he would have. He had been miserable for a long time.

Her Daddy had probably made the smart decision. Life was "the pits" so he checked out. Thoughts like this kept running though her mind. That just made it worse. She would feel guilty because she had hundreds of reasons to feel grateful. She listed them, kept a journal and tried to feel grateful, yet, inevitably, "*So what?*" was her conclusion. Life was a burden. She was too tired to live it and knew no way out. She felt trapped. Emerson was probably right, she thought, *most men live out their lives in quiet desperation.*

In the midst of this gloom, there was one bright spot. With the money from the sale of their house in Arkansas and a small inheritance from Virgil's estate, they built a new home. The furniture they had stored when they first moved to Whitney was set in place. The extra space was heavenly. The view from the deck overlooking Lake Whitney was breathtaking. This view provided some peace and solace for both Donna and Neal.

Chapter 22

Life is not the author of confusion.

June 28, 1981 Donna came home from work to find Neal lying on the deck lounge chair exhausted.

"What's happened?" she asked, terrified.

"I don't know" he replied. "It seemed that someone else was in control of my mind."

"Where's the car? And Molly, the poodle?" she gasped, realizing that something was terribly wrong. Donna had given the adorable poodle to Neal for Christmas, 1976. He fell in love with her immediately.

Shaking his head in confusion, "Let's go see if we can find both," he said.

Little by little they pieced the situation together. Neal had left the house that morning to go to the post office. He had a golf game scheduled at 10:00 a.m. He never made it to the golf course. Instead he headed for the Lake on roads he had never traveled before, driving 100 miles per hour. He turned down one road that led to the lake and drove the car right into the water where the engine died about 30 feet from dry ground. He was disoriented and sweltering in the 100 degree temperature. Somehow he found his way, walking the four miles home.

They drove and looked and looked and drove. No car. No Molly. In desperation they drove over to their friend Joe's house for help. He just happened to be there for a vacation that week. After listening to Neal's description of his wild ride, Joe who had been duck hunting in the area the previous season, led them right to the car. They called and called for Molly. Molly was nowhere to be found. They feared she must have tried to swim from the car and had drowned. After the wrecker pulled the car to town, they returned to the lake and miraculously found a dirty, tired and wet poodle.

Still confused and disoriented, Neal went to the bathroom to take a shower. Donna sat in the chair, stunned by the events. Five minutes, ten minutes, 15 minutes passed and the shower was still running. She came out of her shock and hurried to the bathroom to check on him. The shower was going but Neal was gone. The shower was empty. She found him on the bed with his clothes on, soaking wet, asleep.

Confused, frustrated, frightened Donna felt helpless and alone. She checked every few minutes to see if he was still breathing. Something terrible was happening to him. Her mind created all sorts of insane projections. The night seemed endless.

The next morning the doctor diagnosed Neal's condition as a stroke and recommended he rest and not drive. The following week was filled with madness. Neal was terrified, confused and his behavior was crazy. He carried on long conversations with imaginary people. When he thought he was appropriately dressed, he had failed to put on shoes and socks. He smoked imaginary cigarettes and ate his food with his hands. It seemed that all the connections in his brain were short-circuited. Watching all this insanity, Donna's main feeling was one of pity. There was nothing she could do but watch and be patient with him, which was easy to do because she knew he could not help what he was doing or what was happening. The hard part was to stand by and watch him struggle for a sense of reality. She could not do it for him.

Slowly and gradually his behavior improved. The doctor allowed him to drive short distances. So he did the grocery shopping, went to AA meetings and appeared somewhat normal again. Somewhat normal, was all. Neal was drinking his coffee at the food bar early one morning in the kitchen. On her way into the room she heard Neal desperately mumble, "I must be losing my mind."

A few weeks after his "car in the lake" episode, the cleaning lady quit because Neal had made sexual advances toward her, exposing himself. Donna did not take these episodes very seriously because she felt they were happening as the result of his stroke. She talked to him about his behavior. She told him to not feel guilty about it. It was just part of his sickness. He promised it would never happen again. But it did.

Neal had gone to an AA meeting that Monday night. The phone rang shortly after he had left. It was the new cleaning woman's husband. He was totally enraged that Neal would do such an unspeakable thing to his wife. Neal had exposed himself to her as well. Donna tried to calm him down, explaining that Neal was sick and harmless. He would not hear anything she had to say, ending the conversation by slamming down the phone. When Neal walked in around 9:00 p. m. Donna was sitting at the food bar. He sat down across from her. She quietly said,

"It's happened again."

"What's happened?" he asked.

She told him about the phone call. He denied it and abruptly marched upstairs. Donna followed him. Confused and shaken, they searched for words.

Finally, on the verge of tears, Donna sobbed, "I can't keep from crying."

"I've cried all my life," Neal replied, sadly, biting his lower lip to keep from crying. "I thought the AA program would take care of it. But it didn't."

Donna didn't know what he was talking about. In desperation she suggested, "We need help. Please call Dr. Hill in the morning. Maybe he can refer us to a psychiatrist."

Dr. Hill recommended a psychiatrist in Waco. The following day Neal drove to Waco for a consultation. When he returned home he told Donna that Dr. Winter wanted to talk to her.

"He also wants me to go to the hospital for some tests. He has made arrangements for me to be admitted on Friday."

"I'll do anything. Something is terribly wrong and we need somebody to help us," Donna said hopefully.

The ride to Waco on Friday to see the doctor was grim. There were no words. Each seemed to be in their own world of uncertainty and upheaval. The future was unthinkable.

When Donna sat down in Dr. Winter's office, his first words were, "Mr. Lancaster is very smooth."

A bit surprised by this comment, Donna nodded cautiously.

He continued. "Neal's problem began long before you met him. Neal is a child molester."

Shock was followed by rage. She felt angry, used, abused and deceived. Images and impressions from the past flooded her thoughts. The doctor said nothing while Donna experienced these powerful emotions. Then slowly the picture came into view. It was like there was a huge picture puzzle of their lives on the wall, only there was one piece missing. Dr. Winter had put the piece in place. She could see and remember and knew, knew he was telling her the truth. She recalled the time she saw Neal and the twelve-year-old daughter of friends in Neal's car. The twelve-year-old was driving. Donna had felt an overwhelming stab of pain. Now she knew.

"I don't know if I can stay in the marriage. Can Neal make it alone?"

"We'll have to see. I'll help him all I can," Dr. Winter said.

At the hospital, she helped Neal check in and unpack. His home for the next two weeks would be the psychiatric floor of Providence Hospital. Locked in.

On the way home she started sorting things out.

So that was it. Now she understood why their marriage could be nothing less than perfect. Neal knew and had always known. If there were any bumpy places between them, he would have to look at the one thing he could not bear to look at. It was so despicable, so awful to him that he could not reveal it, not even in the many self-searching inventories the AA had program suggested. They both played the role of "everything is wonderful" and put on the façade, unwilling to admit that their marriage was not perfect. Both were slowly dying. It was not Neal who caused Donna's unhappiness. It was her inability to be open and honest about how she felt. She just couldn't do it. The risk was too great. What risk? Rejection? Disapproval? What would people think? All of this seemed ridiculous now.

With this new information, there was a different twist. She had looked for years for a justification to leave the marriage. Now she could leave and not feel guilty. The very thought of it exhilarated her. But what about Neal? It seemed that he was almost a non-entity at this point. To feel sorry for him would not make him well. It would only make Donna sick. Although she knew that he could not help doing the things he was doing, she also knew there was no treatment. His body was healthy, and the future with him seemed full of torment. Donna reasoned that she was not responsible for him. He was an adult. She did not realize at this point that the tests from the hospital revealed that he suffered from atrophy of the brain. He was mentally incapable of taking care of himself.

Once the decision was made to get a divorce, it was irreversible. Tons of weight seemed to fall away and Donna had a lightness and enthusiasm for living for the first time in many, many years.

Donna spent the weekend looking at the facts and assimilating the shocking information. She drove to Providence Hospital on Monday morning. She was ushered though the locked doors into a small waiting room. The nurses escorted Neal to the visitors' area. He appeared disheveled and confused.

"I'm on my way to an attorney to file for divorce," she said quietly.

"I don't blame you," he replied.

"I've written down a financial settlement, splitting everything right down the middle. My inheritance from my father paid for our house and is not subject to the settlement. We have $20,000 in savings from the sale of the plane. You'll also receive the mortgage payments from the house in Arkansas. Those payments, plus your Social Security will give you over $1000.00 a month. Look this over and see if it's all right with you." She handed him a piece of paper with the figures. "I love you and I'm grateful for our life together. I'm sorry for all the mistakes I've made and for all the times I've hurt you. I love you but I can't live with you any longer. I'll do everything I can to help you adjust to living alone."

Before they could have any more discussion, a nurse came to take Neal for some x-rays. This ended the discussion.

Donna filed for divorce on October 5, 1981. During the next few weeks she found a place for Neal to live and packed his belongings. When he left the hospital his new home was ready. He had enough income to live on, a car to drive and Molly. Donna either saw him daily when they went to meetings or talked to him on the phone. Each time she assured him he could make it. He never complained or objected. He seemed in a complete state of non-resistance. Perhaps the whole process of uncovering his dark secret was more than he could bear. Life was more than he could bear.

The AA and Al-Anon communities were appalled. When someone would ask Donna, "Why a divorce?"

"It's just what I have to do." She was not going to air his problem to others. It was none of their business. She also didn't want Neal to hurt anymore. She really wanted Neal to be whole and healthy. She was blind to the fact that his brain atrophy made wholeness impossible for him. She was not aware of that information until after she had filed for divorce. At that point it seemed too late to change the direction events were propelling her towards. The moment had come and gone. There was no turning back.

On December 14 1981, the divorce was final. They were so friendly and cooperative with each other; the attorney questioned why they were even getting a divorce. They didn't, or couldn't, go into that issue. It was too painful for both of them. Since they were no longer married, they had new wills prepared, which they signed immediately after the divorce decree. Neal left his estate to Donna. Donna left her estate to Neal. They both added a cremation clause. It was as simple as that.

Chapter 23

The only time we want to change anything
is when we think we know the future.

A week before Christmas Donna invited Neal to eat Christmas dinner with her and some friends from the Chapel. He said he had made plans to visit his brother, John and his wife Polly, in Ponca City, Oklahoma. Everyone who knew about his plans wanted him to take a bus, but he insisted on driving the 350 miles. The morning he left he went by the Chapel where Donna was working. They spread out the road map and planned the route for his trip. As he walked out the door, she handed him the map, which he had forgotten to pick up.

He turned and said, "I don't need a map. All I need is God."

He looked so lost and alone. It was all she could do to keep from going with him. She would punish herself many times later because she had let him go, knowing he was in no condition to make the trip alone. He made a wrong turn in Fort Worth and ended up in Cisco, 200 miles in the wrong direction. His car had broken down or who knows where he would have ended up. He called Donna from a motel. They decided to leave the car in Cisco at a garage to be repaired and he would take the bus on to Ponca City. Donna had called Polly and told her what had happened. They were to call when Neal arrived. She heard nothing from them. Finally she called again. Neal had arrived the night before, disoriented, unshaven, confused and lost. John and Polly were angry with Donna for allowing Neal to leave Whitney in such an unstable state.

While he was there, Neal told John and Polly that he had made it clear in his Will that he should be cremated after his death. For some reason, known only to him, he felt the need to deliver this information to his family and he was the only one who could do it.

A few days later he began his trip back to Whitney by bus. He was still disoriented. He could not stay on the bus. In Oklahoma City he got off and called Donna to find someone to come and get him. She did. Jim and Betty lived near Neal. They had been checking on him every day. Jim agreed to drive to Oklahoma City and bring him home.

Throughout the Christmas holidays Donna felt touchy and irritable. Loud noises made her want to scream. She couldn't keep from crying. Something terrible was happening.

Two weeks had passed since the divorce was final.

On Sunday morning, January 3, 1982 Jim stepped into Donna's office after the Chapel service.

"Donna," he said softly, "Betty and I stopped by to check on Neal this morning. Apparently he died in his sleep."

"No! No! No! He can't die. He's going to make it!" The pain was almost unbearable. Guilt. Anger. Sorrow. Grief. Self-condemnation. Emptiness. The emotions were overwhelming. The only relief came from weeping.

The director of the funeral home needed someone to advise him concerning the services. There was no one else to take care of arrangements except Donna. Legally, she was Neal's ex-wife. Emotionally she was his widow. She showed the director Neal's will, which included his instructions to cremate his body. However, Donna was not Neal's wife and she could not sign the necessary papers. The director called John, Neal's brother to confirm the written instructions. Neal had made it to Ponca City and told them his request. Just in time.

Neal's daughter, Lisa, and her fiancé arrived early Monday morning in time for the Memorial Service on Tuesday. Donna and

Lisa shared the information that had been hidden for a long time. Lisa had known for many years about her father's problem. He never touched her, although her stepsisters were still going to counselors regarding their problems related to Neal molesting them.

John and Polly, Neal's sister, Katherine and Donna's brother and sister-in-law, Delbert and Donna came to Whitney for the service. The memorial service was held at the Chapel. The AA community all attended, even though they didn't understand what was going on, they continued to love Neal and Donna. Neal had made an incredible contribution to the lives of hundreds of alcoholics and their families in Whitney, as well as in Siloam Springs. Everyone remembered Neal as loving, considerate, and full of fun and laughter. The service was a celebration of his life. The whole family was comforted.

John, Polly and Katherine were still angry, which was understandable. They felt Donna had abandoned Neal, took all the money and left him to die. When Donna called them, they let her know in no uncertain terms they did not want to communicate with her in any way. Many years later, after John had died, Donna drove to Ponca City and told Polly the whole story. She said,

"I knew there had to be more to it. I'm glad John is gone and never knew."

☘ ☘ ☘

Her greatest comfort came from a surprising source, Elise Lancaster, Neal's ex-wife and mother of Lisa.

Lisa and her mother had moved to Providence, Rhode Island in the early 1960s. Elise was a violinist and taught music. Lisa had been studying cello since early childhood. She applied and was accepted by the Julliard School of Music. She obtained her Master's degree on scholarships and got a position with a prestigious New England string quartet. She continued to be a gifted, enthusiastic artist even after her marriage to Jeff.

Elise wrote Donna a letter. She and Neal were married in 1952. She had two daughters, Lisa's stepsisters, who Neal had molested. They were divorced in 1956, for obvious reasons. Twenty-five years had gone by, yet she took the time to write Donna the following:

Dear Donna,

I just had a long, long phone conversation with Lisa and it left me so moved at what had happened to you---to all of us—through Neal. I had to contact you and tell you that I am glad you are reexamining the whole thing and that I admire you for the way you tried in the way you knew best to support Neal to the end. I feel guilty because I could not.

I think Neal was one of the truly good people under terrible compulsions. God alone can imagine their horrible sources. I feel that Lisa is right and that he has been able to shed some of this with the severing of his body. Who knows? I trust her psychic instincts.

I'm sure you are going through a great deal of suffering and questioning. And right now, it's hard to see that that is good. But knowing you, I'm sure you will come out with gold. Do not worry about people who cannot understand. They are hurt. They could not believe what is really true if they heard. I am sorry they have hurt you. They are afraid.

Donna, if there is anything I can do for you, I would be only too happy.

I am glad that you are questioning everything. We all are. It is a very big question and sometimes I think those that seem the surest, know the least.

My best regards, Elise

Elise was the one person in the whole world (except maybe the psychiatrist) who knew the whole, ugly story. The letter was like a soothing balm on shattered and raw emotions. Donna read and re-read the letter hungry to soak up the love, understanding and compassion Elise had expressed. This gift she gave Donna was beyond measure.

Chapter 24

Life is always trying to wake us up.

Guilt still enveloped Donna like a shroud. Memories crowded her mind, most of them sad. She remembered only the times when she had failed him, failed to listen and understand or failed to reach out and touch his hurting heart. She felt like she had deserted her best friend. In his own way, Neal was screaming for help. In her stubborn and self-serving way, she had stood there, unmoving, watching him fade away. The guilt was devastating.

Her sick and battered emotions convinced her the divorce was a tragic mistake. Perhaps she had even killed him. She had prayed, meditated and lit candles. She had even coordinated a Chapel for Him. That alone should have guided her life. God should have told her Neal was going to die. She would have stayed with him. She didn't want Neal to die. She wanted him to make it. She *knew* he would make it. But he didn't. Evidently there was no such thing as inner guidance. She had been betrayed into believing something that was not true. She was enraged.

Something happened that made her aware of her anger. She and several friends were eating in a restaurant. A baby at the table next to them was crying. Donna remarked, "If that kid doesn't stop screaming, I'm going to kill it!" Whoa! This rage was something she had better deal with—now!

Immediately upon arriving home, she grabbed a pillow and found the tennis racket. With great gusto she began beating the pillow with every ounce of energy she had. She thought of everything and everybody she was or had been angry with and pictured their faces on the pillow and beat, beat, beat, saying all the mean, ugly things she had ever wanted to say. She screamed out everything she had bottled up for years. This went on for a long time because there were many and the more she beat, the more anger she remembered. She finally included herself in this tirade, berating herself for the mess she had made of her life and the self-hatred that was slowly destroying her. Then the big one: God had done it to her. So, with all the energy she could muster, she pictured God on the pillow, and struck Him, over and over. With one crashing blow of the tennis racket, she killed Him.

It was over. She had probably never been this honest. The God in the sky, the cosmic scorekeeper was dead, gone. Evidently there was no one to answer her prayers, give comfort, or give any indication that Life was a worthwhile adventure. Any concepts of God, Life, Joy, Life-Everlasting, were shattered. She stood alone. There never had been, nor was there now, anyone up there who rewarded her when she was good or punished her when she was bad. There was no one out there to answer her pleas for help. Suddenly an overwhelming sense of peace and freedom enfolded her.

The old rigid belief system that had held her in bondage had crumbled. Her ego had tried to believe in God, Jesus, the Bible or the twelve steps because it was a safe harbor. It's better to be safe, even though it's not true, than to stand naked and alone. But the price had become too high. She could no longer pretend to be a believer. She knew nothing, believed nothing. All her preconceived opinions had vanished like the illusions they really were. She felt a sense of joy that was indescribable. She knew nothing or believed in anything, not even herself. Life was one big joke. But the conflict was gone. The negative emotions were gone. Emptiness was a far more desirable state than conflict. She also knew only one thing: She was entirely responsible for the state of her being and her life. This was a relief, but it was also a challenge.

There was no one or anything to blame if she was happy, unhappy, sad, depressed or any of the other many states. She was responsible. Period. With this realization came great freedom. She didn't have to wait anymore for the world and/or the people in it to change in order for her to be happy.

She could now leave the Chapel. She had been doing it to please God anyway. It was a tremendous relief to know God couldn't care less. Opportunities were out there. It was time to start looking.

Chapter 25

We cannot control circumstances or how other people treat us.
We can choose our responses to circumstances.

The following months passed peacefully. Donna still didn't know anything other than she was alive. The past was gone, only an illusion in the recesses of her mind. The future was an unwritten page, waiting for her to write the daily script. The ego mind wanted to know the future so it could make arrangements to be comfortable. The ego mind wanted the security of knowing. But that was not to be at this time, so it finally quit its clamoring. The peace and quiet were most welcome.

In June, Donna flew commercially to New York to visit an old friend, Betty, for a few days. Her home in Brooklyn Heights, was close to everything. While Betty was at work, Donna hiked to the local grocery story without her tall legs. She strolled the promenade, a walkway that overlooked Manhattan, and visited with the people resting on the benches.

She wrote in her journal:

Betty left for work early this morning. We had discussed the groceries we needed for our evening meal. I wanted to do the shopping because she would come home tired, hungry and late. I had planned to use my crutches to go to the store, yet to carry a sack of groceries and walk at the same time was very difficult. She heard a conversation start in her head: you can carry the groceries without your legs on, so don't wear them. Besides, who cares, but you?

These thoughts made her heart beat faster. Could she really face the world outside again as a short person? She knew that someday she'd have to resolve this issue. She knew that as she aged the weight of the legs were physically taking a toll on her body. But today? She broke out in a sweat and her pulse was pounding. The fear was uncanny.

Dressed in her size one moccasins, slacks for her little legs and her favorite blue sweatshirt, she opened the door of Betty's home and stepped into the world. The door clicked shut behind her. A wave of fear hit her, then passed. She had to tilt her head upward to smile and speak to everyone she met, and friendly eyes spoke back to her. A few people would not consent to eye contact, but she didn't take it personally. Those few would not have looked at Joe Blow or Mary Doe, either.

She skipped the two blocks to the grocery store and pushed the shopping cart through the aisles, the handle of the cart above her head. She asked clerks or other shoppers to hand her the items she couldn't reach. She was surprised how eager they were to help her. She absorbed the warmth and friendliness of these strangers. It seemed the cocoon of self-absorption and self-concern she had lived in for so long was breaking away. She was allowing herself to feel the outside world and she was finding it to be a very loving and gentle place.

"I wonder why I keep wearing these heavy old legs?" she questioned. "I certainly have more physical freedom. Besides they're cumbersome. What is it that keeps me tied into them, day after day, year after year, I wonder?" The time was coming when she would have to confront these perplexing questions.

On the way to Whitney from DFW Airport, she stopped at the Cleburne Airport, thirty-five miles north of Whitney, to see her friends Sam and Betty Ball. They operated the airport and were helpful to Donna when she had her plane tied down on their ramp. In their visit, Sam told Donna that he was looking for someone to do some of the office paperwork and shop billing. Donna was immediately interested. It sounded like a lot more fun to be around planes and pilots than to set up boring seminars and Sunday Services.

"I'd like to apply for the job," Donna offered.

"I can't pay very much," Sam countered. "I can only pay $5.00 a hour. I'm sure you make more than that now."

"I don't care. If you'll hire me and teach me what I need to know, I want the job." She earnestly pleaded.

"You've got it," Sam smiled. "When can you start?"

"I'll turn in my resignation tomorrow and give them a month to find someone to replace me. How about July 15th?"

That was fine with him.

"Wow! I get to work at an airport. I get to work in the magic world of aviation! What an opportunity!" She sang all the way home.

Sam was a patient teacher. She discovered he didn't like to do shop billing, sending out statements to the owners for labor and parts on their aircraft. Sam was a year behind, amounting to thousands of dollars. The mechanics would write their hours on their time cards. On the back of their time cards, they would list the parts from the parts room they had used for each aircraft. That was all the information available. From that data an invoice was generated. It was like being a detective in a high profile crime scene. She loved it. In three months, Sam's shop billing was up to date. Sam had other projects for her to do, but some things had developed she needed to consider.

When they moved to Texas in 1979, she had studied for and passed the broker's exam for the State of Texas. She called Don and Karen Maloney who owned an agency to see if they could use another agent. They met at their Real Estate office on Sunday afternoon. It was they, not Donna, who brought up the subject of whether or not she needed to wear her legs. They just didn't care if she was short or tall. She could wear her artificial legs or not wear them. They wanted her to be comfortable. It was not an issue to them. It was her decision. Their open willingness to hire her, short or tall, surprised Donna.

What was going on? Only last evening she was visiting with her friend, Glenda. Sitting on the floor playing cards, Donna needed to go to the bathroom. With the artificial legs on, the effort to stand up was considerable.

Glenda casually remarked, "Why do you keep wearing those heavy legs? You don't need to wear them."

"I have to wear them," Donna replied defensively. Glenda recognized she had touched a nerve, smiled and dropped the subject.

But maybe she didn't have to wear them. She was fully functional without them. In fact, she was much more agile and mobile without them. She had worn them for thirty-two years. She had never seriously considered *not* wearing them. They were a part of her daily routine. She had put her legs on each morning just as others put on their shoes or panty hose. She loved this tall world where she could see others at their level. She loved coordinating the clothes, shoes and blazers. She felt like she looked good when she marched off to work. She was fifty-one years old. Was the price in energy and mobility she paid to function in the legs becoming too high?

One of her justifications for wearing them had fallen apart when Don and Karen hired her to sell Real Estate for them, with or without the legs. She had wondered if she would be hired for *any* position as a short person. Obviously, her height was not a big deal. They were only interested in her performance as an agent. She could certainly move about much more easily without the ten pounds laced on each leg. Steps were difficult. Carrying anything took precision and balance. So what was it that tied her to them, day after day? Ego? Vanity? Pride? What will people think? These were flimsy reasons to punish her body with this needless, strenuous pursuit. These mental conversations continued for several days.

Of course there wasn't any God to help her sort it out.

Dr. Bob Gibson, a Master Teacher and at one time a practicing psychiatrist, was a regular guest speaker at the Chapel. As her mentor, he had told her,

"Donna, people don't care if you're short or tall. They love you anyway. And remember, we can all deal with what is."

"What is?" Donna was jarred, remembering that conversation. "What is?" Of course. For thirty-two years she had been trying to change "what is" into "what she thought it ought to be." She was short. She was embarrassed to be short. Being tall like other people removed most of her discomfort. She was at a turning point. Which way held the least discomfort? To be tall, safe, yet physically stressed? Or to be short and emotionally uncomfortable? It was time to do what was to her advantage, regardless of the pain and clamoring ego.

Okay, she told herself, I'll just go to the Real Estate office short. For everything else I'll be tall. That sounded reasonable. Deep down she knew that sooner or later she would have to set the legs aside. She might as well get it over with. The decision was made. She would start her new job at Maloney Realty the following day–short.

She had no idea, fortunately, what challenges lay before her.

Chapter 26

Are we grown-up enough not to be controlled by emotions?

The night was restless. Fear seemed to cling to her like a shroud. She was surprised. It sounded simple enough. Just walk out of the house in the morning without those heavy legs, climb easily into the car, and drive handily to work. She was shocked to feel the fear immobilize her. What made this simple transition such a big deal?

Morning finally came. Her wardrobe was tailored to clothe a towering 5'8" woman. What could she wear? It was early November and she would need a jacket. Did she have any jackets or sweaters short enough to not drag the floor? She found a green pullover velour V-necked sweater. Around the house she had been wearing a pair of green plaid short pants she had cut down from longer ones. These would match the sweater. And finally, a pair of moccasins for her tiny size-one feet.

Even though the fear was still there, she never considered throwing in the towel. At any moment she could lace on the tall legs and call the whole thing off. The decision she had made to face this transition was deep and strong enough to be in charge, regardless of what her emotions were doing. She put one foot in front of the other and walked to the car. Drops of perspiration oozed from every pore. She felt naked, vulnerable, paranoid, insecure and scared.

She opened the door to the Real Estate office. Most of her co-workers had never seen her short. Their surprise was obvious. Just as thirty-two years before everyone was shocked to see Donna twenty inches taller, they now were seeing her twenty inches shorter. They couldn't help responding with shock and surprise. The change was drastic.

There was another difference. Thirty-two years ago the experience of suddenly being 5'8" was exhilarating. The excitement and fun of being tall wiped out all the hardships and difficulties. Now, Donna did not want to be short. But, she also knew that the time had come to set the legs aside and not be tall anymore. The conflict was overwhelming and she ended up having the worst cold she could ever remember.

By noon things were a bit easier. All the agents climbed into Don's wagon to drive around and look at new listings. Her fellow agents didn't know whether to lift her into the wagon, offer to help or just watch as she lifted herself onto the seat. This different Donna was a new experience for all of them.

The freedom of mobility was starting to sink in. How easy it was to step up on a curb or climb stairs or jump into a car or run into the store without dragging twenty inches and twenty pounds along with her. This did indeed make the physical effort to function incredibly easier.

But her ego was not going to let her off the hook easily. It was not ready to give up the idea that the tall legs made her feel okay about herself. She felt as if pain oozed from every cell in her body. Many nights she woke up and the sheets would be soaked with perspiration, thinking, "I must be losing my mind."

She called Dr. Bob for some guidance. He told her, "Donna, you're playing roles. If you're short, play the role of a short person to the hilt. When you're tall, play the tall role to the hilt. Don't make the change too quickly."

That sounded reasonable. She would sell Real Estate six days a week and play the short role. Each Wednesday she drove to the Cleburne Airport to do Sam's shop billing. On that day she laced on her legs and played the tall role. Betty and Sam didn't know until the next April that she was short the other six days of the week. She felt like two different people. Maybe I'm schizophrenic, she thought.

Everything seemed hopeless. She looked in the closet for something to wear--and burst into tears. If she was going to stick with this decision to be short she had better alter some clothes to wear. She selected four pair of slacks, cut off 20 inches and began hemming them up. Trips to the clothing stores only deepened the despair. She would walk through the racks of beautiful clothes, then run to the fitting room and weep.

On the way home one evening, the despair was overwhelming. She decided to stop by to see Tanya, her best friend. She pulled into the driveway, but couldn't get out of the car.

Tanya came out and sat in the car, holding Donna while she cried. Then she said, "Donna, with your artificial legs on, you're handicapped. With your legs off, you're exceptional."

Those precious words continued to give her strength and encouragement in the days and months ahead.

Attending the office Christmas party was as unthinkable as climbing Mt Everest.

Clothes were the big objection, although this was only a cover-up for her feelings of not being "okay." Tanya's husband was a fellow agent and they would be going to the party. Tanya reassured her,

"Donna, this is the perfect time to step out socially. You'll be with all the people who love and support you."

At that moment, Donna said, "Okay, I'm going." In the next moment, "No, I can't do it." The resistance was intense. There were no pretty clothes to wear and appropriate shoes for her little feet were impossible. She could have worn her legs and been tall, but she didn't want to do that, either.

The evening turned out to be delightful. No one cared whether she was short or tall. She could easily see all of the turmoil and conflict was within her. It had nothing to do with anyone else. She alone was responsible for how she perceived things. She could continue in this pitiful, hardheaded, stubborn mode or she could drop it. No one or no thing was causing her to be miserable. She was writing the script. She could re-write it anytime she wanted to.

Some adjustments had to be made at work. As a Real Estate agent she talked to clients at her desk before taking them on a property tour. She discovered that if they didn't know she was short (which they couldn't know when she sat behind her desk) they would be surprised when she jumped down out of her chair. It was much easier on everyone if she greeted her clients at the door, introduced herself and asked them to have a seat. This gave them a few minutes to adjust to her height and she didn't loose their attention as potential buyers when she slid out of her chair later.

She was overly self-conscious about her physical appearance. This attitude was self-defeating and non-productive. In an effort to overcome this self-centeredness, she contacted the local Avon lady about becoming a representative. A territory was open near her house. Armed with the Avon sample kit and order pad she proceeded to become acquainted with her neighbors.

Intentions were easy. Actions were more difficult. She would lie on the couch after supper, dreading making the calls. In order to pry herself off the couch, she made a pact that she only had to make three calls a night and reminded herself that in one hour it would all be over. The resistance was heavy. She crawled out of the house, into the car and down the street—without letting her mind be in control. She found everyone friendly. Many were lonely and welcomed someone to visit with. They usually bought something so she would come back to see them when their order arrived. This wonderful response from others was refreshing and uplifting.

Then something happened that refocused the whole picture.

Chapter 27

A peaceful mind doesn't want to change anything.

The February evening was warm, warm enough to sit on the deck overlooking the lake and watch the sunset. As long as she kept her mind on something interesting, she was much happier. In periods of silence, the same old questions bubbled up; none of which seemed to have an answer. This time it was different. The brown wren was bellowing out its magnificent melody. Suddenly, Donna heard it. Really heard it. "What is it in me that takes those musical vibrations and transforms them into meaning and beauty?" she asked. "There's no sound until they hit my ears."

She then saw the sunset with its array of gold, pink and lavender.

Again she asked, "What is it in me that takes those color vibrations and changes the vibration into beauty and elegance?" In that moment she knew there was something invisible and intangible within her that lived. The finite mind could not define this essence, but it did answer the question, "What am I? I am an expression of infinite Life."

It could be called by many names, God, Life, Essence, Spirit, Allah, Buddha, Intelligence, Love. She didn't know what all of this would mean, but there was a definite shift in the value she placed on her existence. She was so much more than she thought she was—it boggled her mind. And if she were more, so also, was everyone else.

She sat there a long, long time, feeling the warmth of her skin.

She listened to her breathing and her heart beating.

"There is something in me that hears, sees, digests food, creates. I can do none of those things. I can't even grow one hair on my head or grow a fingernail. There is *Something* within me so magnificent there are no words to define it." She was spellbound.

From that moment on there was no more doubt. She didn't know what it was all about, and she didn't need to know. She was at peace with the fact of her existence. There was no longer any urge to change anything or anybody, including herself. The Creative Spirit was far more intelligent than she was. She could wholeheartedly embrace Life on Life's terms.

Life took on a different texture. The conflict and resistance to every "what is" was gone. She knew that she was on a journey of some sort and that Life loved her so much that it would bring into her experience everything she needed.

She was at peace.

Chapter 28

Real prayer is praying for wisdom.

In the winter of 1983 she received a call from some friends in Dallas. They had heard about a new airfreight company just starting up and it was going to hire only women pilots. If she was interested, they had a phone number to call for more information.

She wasted no time. She called immediately and asked them to send her an application, which they did. When she dropped the application into the mail she thought, "Wouldn't it be great to have a job doing what I love to do most–flying."

In a few weeks, the company called to set up an interview.

Now came the big question. Should she go to the interview short or tall? She was at a turning point. Short or tall? She decided it would probably be to her advantage to be tall. After all, this was a big event and an opportunity of a lifetime. She wanted to make the most of it and put her best foot forward, which would be her wooden foot. Since she still didn't have any satisfactory clothes to wear, she could at least dress appropriately with the legs on.

She gathered up her logbooks and FAA certificates and headed for Love Field in Dallas.

Everyone was very warm and friendly. They had four Piper Malibu's on order. These were single engine planes with a healthy payload. They would be flying freight, mostly at night and in all kinds of weather. Most of the interview was about what they were planning and not about her at all. They said they would call.

Weeks went by. She continued to sell Real Estate – short, and work at Sam's on Wednesdays—tall. In February they called for her to come for another interview.

By this time she was more comfortable without the artificial legs.

"Shall I go to the interview short or tall?" she questioned. If they hired her, they would know sooner or later that she was short.

"I might as well face it now, rather than later."

A classy friend, Fran Hillen, was visiting her from Midland that week. On the morning of the interview they spent time arranging the new red skirt and matching blouse under a short jacket, along with a small over-the-shoulder purse. Shoes were still a problem for her small feet, so she had to make due with her moccasins. All in all, she looked rather good. Not like other people, but with what she had to work with, she looked decent.

She was a bit anxious on the drive to Dallas.

"I guess if they don't want someone my size flying their planes, now is a good time to settle this issue."

There was one problem with wearing a skirt. A long stairway led to the executive offices. If anyone was behind her, they could see right up her little short dress. She waited until the stairway was clear, then dashed up the steps.

The interview went well. They hired her. The fact that she had dissolved from 5'8" to 3'10" was never mentioned, perhaps not even noticed. They couldn't have cared less.

The chief pilot, Marilyn, another pilot and Donna all went out to lunch. The restaurant they chose was Celebration where all of the executives went for lunch. Donna was so relieved and excited that she was at her best. This was truly a celebration. When the tasty meal was over, Donna tried to push her seat back, so she could climb down out of the chair. However, the chair wouldn't push back. It pushed over and then she toppled over, bottom up and feet in the air. A hundred pair of startled eyes settled on her position on the floor. Donna leveled her gaze on Marilyn and smiled, saying, "Hell of a way to impress my new employer."

Thank goodness they could all laugh about it.

Initially, she was to start on May 1, 1984. This was delayed a month until June 1st. During May, she and Tanya spent days in Dallas apartment hunting. They settled on the last place they looked at, not because it was anything special, but because it was the last place on the list. They were tired and it was a good as any. She would be the first tenant in #136 of the new apartment complex.

The kitchen was handy, with a large walk-in pantry. The large bedroom also had a walk-in closet, and the living room had patio doors, looking out on a small concrete, fenced area. Donna filled out the application and paid first and last month's rent. It was just beginning to dawn on her that she was moving to Dallas. There was a lot ahead of her. Rent the lake house. Have a garage sale. Pack. Decide what to do with Molly. Leaving the comfort and ease of lake living was never even a thought, at least now.

Chapter 29

A quiet mind is impossible if we are making anything important.

She found someone to rent the house furnished, which simplified the packing. The garage sale went well and she got rid of everything she wouldn't need. She was not sentimental over things, and could trim her possessions down to the essentials. She would take the game table and chairs, the couch, a bed and chest, clothes, dishes—and her two pair of legs, just in case.

. Molly, her precious poodle, was not an easy decision. Molly was her companion, comforter and best friend. They had been through a lot together. She knew she would be flying and away from home. What was best for each of them? Her next-door neighbor, Alma, helped her with this tough one. She asked Donna,

"What has more value in your life? Molly or your new job?"

The answer was obvious. She would have to find Molly a good home. This was so painful she could hardly think about it. All of a sudden the same feelings she had had about Neal surfaced. When he died, she felt she had deserted him, her best friend. Now, faced with leaving Molly, these same feelings came rushing back. She started weeping and couldn't seem to stop. When it was finally over, she knew what she had to do. Her friend, Lucille, had kept Molly from time to time when Donna had to leave town for a day or two. She would provide a wonderful, loving home for her.

Tanya's husband had a pickup and three other friends wanted to help. On Thursday, May 31, they loaded up the truck and headed for Dallas. It was late afternoon before they had deposited all the furniture and boxes in the new apartment. They left her, cheerfully waving and calling, "Have fun. Lots of luck."

Needing some groceries to begin her new life, she drove to the store and picked up milk, eggs and bread. On the way home a boy ran a stoplight and smashed into her car.

Her first thought was not, "Is anybody hurt?" but, "How can I get to work on Monday without a car to drive? I can't drive just anybody's car. I have to have hand-controls."

The police finally came. The boy was given a ticket, and, of course, didn't have any insurance. The officer asked her what wrecker service and repair place she wanted to use.

"I have no idea. Can you help me? I've lived here only one hour."

He was very gracious and called a wrecking service at the Buick auto shop to tow her car away. He loaded her and her groceries, covered with slimy broken eggs into his car, and drove her to her new apartment.

This was not what she had in mind. No phone. No car. Nothing could be done until morning. So she started unpacking boxes. This kept her from creating numerous scenarios, all of which would be illusions and a waste of energy. By midnight she was unpacked and tired enough to fall immediately asleep.

Since her phone would not be connected until later in the day, she used the phone in the apartment's business office. Her first call was to the insurance company. The information that they had for her was fantastic. Avis Rental Car could put hand controls on cars. Whoopee! Her greatest concern was transportation. Her apartment was 13 miles from Love Field. A car was not a luxury, but a necessity. She called Avis at DFW Airport. They would have a car ready for her by 2:00 p.m. She couldn't have been more pleased and excited. All of the other situations she would have to deal with amounted to nothing at all. She had a car she could drive. Everything would work out.

Well, so she thought until Monday morning.

134

Chapter 30

Life sets up all sorts of situations so we can learn.

The freight company had hired about twenty female pilots for their operation. They gathered in the executive office to receive their initial briefing. They were all excited about the opportunity to do what they loved most and get paid for it—fly. The CEO came into the room, rather soberly.

Her first comment was, "I have some distressing news. The finances for this operation have been withdrawn. We are no longer in business."

The silence was almost tangible. Some of the pilots had moved to Dallas from other states. They had quit jobs, left their friends or family, given their pets away and had made major adjustments, just as Donna had done. They were stunned, then angry. Watching the groups of women complain and whine about their situation, Donna knew whining was not the answer. Her mother had taught her that little gem forty years ago when she whined about washing the dishes. She didn't know what she'd do. Maybe the Ramada would hire her as a maid. She was just the right height to be a whiz at making beds. She had to get out of this office, before she got pulled into the self-defeating, victim energy that was emerging.

Just as she started out the door, Marilyn, the chief pilot, approached her.

"Donna, I understand Jet East is looking for an aircraft dispatcher. You might want to check it out."

"Aircraft dispatcher? Well, it might be better than cleaning rooms at the Ramada. Thanks for the tip."

Aircraft dispatcher? She had no idea what that meant. It must have something to do with airplanes and that always captured her attention. If she had been asked to write down a hundred things that she would be interested in, aircraft dispatcher would not have been on the list. She was glad she had discarded goal setting years ago. She found it was much too stressful. If her mind had been set on a pilot job, she might have missed this opportunity of a lifetime. So she marched to Jet East, résumé in hand, and asked to see the chief pilot. Ched Bart, the chief pilot, was standing at the door of the break room. Evidently some of the other pilots who had been hired and were now jobless had already been to Jet East looking for a job. He was cool and unfriendly. He did not ask Donna to come to his office or sit down. She stood there uncomfortably.

"I understand you're looking for a dispatcher. I want to apply for the job." Donna offered. "Here's my résumé."

They both remained standing. Ched began reading the résumé. Silence. Finally, he suggested they sit on the couch and talk.

Jet East was a full service, aircraft fixed-base operator. They provided fuel, aircraft maintenance, avionics, aircraft interiors and an impressive fleet of corporate aircraft to charter. At the time the fleet consisted of 6 Lear Jet 35, 3 Lear Jet 25, one Challenger, 2 King Airs, one Falcon 20 and a Citation III. Forty pilots were needed to crew these planes.

The personnel in charter sales took phone calls for those wanting to charter a plane. Then a plane was selected and a crew was briefed. This all sounded simple. But the amount of information necessary to handle this was overwhelming. This included knowing which pilots could fly which aircraft. Some of this data also included distance of flight, time of flight, fuel consumption, runway lengths, hours of airport operations all over the country, airport restrictions, customs, catering, and, especially, how they were going to pay for the trip. A flight from Love Field to Los Angeles and back in a Lear Jet was over $8000.

Donna sat spellbound as Ched explained all of this to her. Finally, he asked, "Would you be available to talk with the Director of Operations and President of Jet East tomorrow?"

She had nothing else to do. "Of course," she said.

The interviews the next day went well. They wanted her to start to work the next morning. Salary was not discussed. She didn't care what it was and didn't bring up the subject. She was just thankful to have a job.

The dispatch room was called the activity and energy center. One entire wall, over twenty feet, was one huge blackboard. The days were at the top, covering two weeks of future charter trips. Along the left side of the board were all the different aircraft. Each block was filled in with the information regarding that particular flight: Destination, times of departure, catering, crew, number of passengers, crew briefings. Each piece of information had to be confirmed on the day preceding the flight.

Ched reminded Donna that they were dealing with very wealthy clients. Mistakes were not tolerated.

"If I don't do this the way you want me to, let me know. I'm a big girl and I can take it," Donna said.

Those words would come back to haunt her.

Chapter 31

Whenever we make anything important,
we are always anxious.

For a few days she sat and watched the activity. It was overwhelming. All the pilots looked alike. She didn't know a King Air from a Lear Jet. She had none of the information that seemed to be required to just answer the telephone, which was always ringing. She left work each evening dazed and exhausted. Self-doubt gnawed at her. "Maybe I'm not bright enough to learn this." She sensed their expectations and hers far exceeded her capacity to absorb all she needed to know.

At the end of the month, Ched called her into his office. "We're going to see how big a girl you are."

Donna sat there silently as Ched enumerated all the things she had been doing wrong. Some were true. Some were not. He informed her she would be re-evaluated in two weeks. If things hadn't changed by then, they would have to replace her. The hole in her stomach was as big as his office.

When he finished, she said quietly, "Thank you for talking to me. I'll redouble my efforts and do the very best I can."

When she climbed in her car she burst into tears.

"This is the most wonderful job I've ever had. By God, I'm going to do this if it kills me."

It nearly did.

She began taking books and schedules home at night to memorize. She memorized the aircraft tail numbers and matched them with who could fly them. She studied FAA regulations concerning charter operations and what they could do or not do. She screamed in the car on the way to work when fear almost paralyzed her. When the tension in the dispatch room was high, she went to the bathroom and did breathing exercises.

By the end of the second month she had shingles.

For several weeks she had had an intense pain in her back. She thought she had pulled a muscle. At night, unable to sleep, she took hot baths, used ice packs, tried to watch TV, or drove to the grocery store, which was open all night. She sat in the middle of the bed reciting poetry or the 23rd Psalm. She was taking four aspirin and four extra-strength Tylenol every two hours. Lack of sleep was taking its toll.

After two weeks of this nightmare, she told Ched on Friday, "I have a doctor's appointment this afternoon. I need to leave a little early."

She drove to the Lake to see Wesley, her friend and chiropractor. She told him what was happening. He told her, "Donna, you have shingles."

"No, I can't have shingles," she sobbed.

"You have a very stressful job. I suggest you quit. We can treat the shingles, but if you continue to be under stress, there will be another physical adaptation."

"Wesley, I can't quit. This is the most wonderful job I've ever had. I want you to help me stay in the job and not let it make me sick."

He had no answer.

The renters at her lake house had moved out and she could stay at the Lake house over the weekend. She had a prescription for pain filled and spent the weekend in bed. By Sunday afternoon, she felt much better and returned to Dallas.

She didn't take any medicine while she was working. The atmosphere in the dispatch room was so intense she felt no pain at work.

The two weeks probation had passed and Ched had said nothing to her. She was not going to bring up her status, because she didn't want to know. It was easier to live in the unknown than to face failure. She did the best she knew how. She could at least operate the computers and give charter quotes to those who called. The people were starting to have names she could remember. The flip charts she had made were helping her tie things together. She had to memorize the planes, their N numbers, who owned them, the owner's secretary's name and what kind of liquor they wanted on board.

The pilots couldn't have been nicer. They were a delightful group of young men who loved to fly more than anything else, just like Donna. At Jet East they could build up their hours and go on to the airlines. Jet East was a classy place and hired a classy group of pilots. She loved them all.

It took one year of learning before Donna felt comfortable in dispatch. If she didn't have the answer, she at least knew where to find it. She was always ready to go to work and Ched never said another word to her.

Years later when he left Jet East for another job, Donna told him, "Ched, I want to thank you for what you did for me. You forced me to dig in and do it. You pulled my very best out of me. It was a great gift."

Chapter 32

Reverence for all life.

There were a few bright spots in those stressful early days at Jet East. She hadn't lived in Dallas very long when Tanya called one evening to see how she was getting along. "What are you doing?" she asked.

"I'm sitting here reading the phone book," Donna replied cheerfully.

"Reading the phone book. Have you gone mad?" With millions of listings in the Dallas area, this seemed rather pointless. She proceeded with caution. "What is that all about?"

"Well, I didn't make it to the library before it closed. So I picked up the phone book. You'd be amazed at the plethora of information they put in it. Schools, civic events, maps, points of interest, etc. It's fascinating reading. I thought I'd get acquainted with this city I'm now living in. Besides it's much more interesting than anything I can find on TV."

It sounded so funny they both started laughing hysterically.

Another bright spot in Donna's new life was Harrison. Hungry for a bit of companionship in her Dallas apartment, she accepted a baby finch from friends who had just had a new crop of them. Donna named him Harrison, her grandfather's middle name. He wore the name proudly.

Harrison Lancaster was about four inches long with a circle of orange on each cheek, a bright red beak and a voice that carried for blocks. He was full of conversation, most of it meaningless chatter.

His hearing was acute, and he had much to say about any insignificant noise. He brightened the house with his squeaky early morning songs. He was also a persistent teacher.

For instance, the time came for Harrison to have a new cage. The old one was rusty and had bird droppings all over it. The new cage was a bit larger and arranged differently. The food cup was in a different place. The round perches were stretched inside the cage at different angles. A new bathing tub was installed. A new swing hung from the top of the cage. Naturally, he was scared and didn't want to be touched. He flew frantically around in his old cage for several minutes before she could hold him long enough to put him in the new cage.

For the first twelve hours he sat in a corner and pouted. He did not like the new cage. He wanted his old familiar, comfortable one where everything was convenient. The new swing threatened him and the new perches required risky flights to reach. Out of necessity he found his food and water. He would not venture any farther from his safe corner. After twenty-four hours he could hit three perches in his circle around the cage, briefly touching his new swing on the way. It took him three days to conquer his favorite perch, his swing. He was teaching Donna that change is an adjustment and a process. Accept being uncomfortable for a while. It will pass.

At this point Donna needed the lesson. Her uncomfortable level was off the charts. She had a nagging feeling that it would never be any different. Watching Harrison gave her the comfort of knowing, "This too, will pass." And it did.

The time came for Harrison to have a female roommate; her name was Harriet. Harriet seemed crazy about him, so they set up housekeeping. With a bit of encouragement, such as putting nesting material and a bamboo nest in their cage, Harrison and Harriet proceeded to start a family. They padded the entire inside of the nest with cotton. Harriet laid three eggs the size of M&M's™. They took turns sitting on them. Each day they turned the eggs over to keep the delicate membrane on the inside of the shell from sticking to it. In twelve days the eggs hatched. For the next twelve days the tiny birds were fed and watered by their attentive parents who patiently filled each tiny beak with nestling food and water. When the three birds (two boys and one girl) emerged from the nest, they were nearly the size of their parents.

Neither Harriet nor Harrison had ever taken a parenting course or read a book on *How to Raise Baby Finch.* Innately they had all the information they needed. Although they had no self-awareness, the techniques for survival operated effortlessly. They did not complain or blame. They did not argue about who was going to feed the kids in the middle of the night or blame each other because we have all these mouths to feed. They did not worry about whether they were doing it right. They just did it. The Life within each of them knew how to do it all.

Donna had forgotten that Life, the Essence within her, was fully operational and contained great wisdom needed for each encounter. She had made it extremely important to be successful at Jet East, leaving her exhausted, fearful and anxious. The Truth was that "Nothing is Important." The world was doing fine before she got here and would do fine after she left the planet. So, how important was she in this whisper of time? If they fired her, so what? Life would go on. Harrison and Harriet lived in the present moment, doing what was before them to do, without worry or anxiety. If their babies died, they would feel no guilt or regret. They had given their best. Could Donna do likewise? Absolutely.

Knowing the Truth does set us free.

Part of the mating ritual involved Harrison pecking on Harriet's neck. He was so persistent she developed bleeding wounds that wouldn't heal. They had to be put in separate cages. When Harrison objected to this arrangement, Donna explained to him that due to his aggressiveness, it was his own fault he was living alone. Harriet died of her wounds. Harrison lived to be 14 years old, which is a very long life for a finch. He had enriched

Donna's life beyond measure.

Chapter 33

We live in that which we radiate.

In 1989 Donna moved from the apartment to a prestigious thirty-two story high rise, only five miles from Love Field. She had friends living in the Preston Tower who had invited her to their apartment several times. The skyline from their windows was fabulous.

"I wonder if I can afford to live here? This really suits my style!" she dreamed. At the urging of her friends she contacted a Real Estate agent.

"Do you have any units for rent?" she inquired.

They did, and she made an appointment to look at several. The first one she saw was just right. On the eighth floor the view was outstanding. The floor to ceiling windows facing south from the living room and bedroom opened from each onto a five by thirty-five foot balcony. There were lots of closets, thick plush carpets, eight- foot ceilings, instant hot water from the hot water faucet and a self-cleaning oven. The building offered valet service, underground parking and exquisite décor. The package became more appealing when she discovered Wednesday night bridge games. She decided to take the risk for one year. If she had any trouble making rent payments, by the end of the year, she would move. Meanwhile, she would embrace high-rise living to the fullest.

Tanya came up from the Lake to help her pack, move and arrange her new home. Tanya was her best friend. Tanya had always been there for her even though many of the times had been painful and miserable. This time it was different. There was joy and fun and laughter. During the packing she would ask: "Do you need this? Do you use this?"

If the answers were no, it went in the trash. No argument. Out it went. They laughed hysterically. With Tanya's knack for decorating and Donna's checkbook, the new apartment was fit for a princess. She truly felt like one.

One of the ladies she played bridge with asked her one afternoon, "Do you know of anyone who would like a part time job with the oil company on the second floor?"

At this time she was working nights at Jet East. She went to work at 4:00 p.m., left Jet East at midnight, or when she finished the work. If there were charter calls during the night, the calls were patched through to her at home. Some nights she might have several calls and maybe a flight or two to arrange. Southwest Organ Bank used Jet East Lear Jets to transport hearts, lungs and kidneys all over the country. These flights were usually at night, because that was when the operating room facilities at the hospitals were available. The donating patients were on life support until the Southwest Organ Bank team of nurses and doctors came for the organs. As dispatcher, Donna made all the arrangements for these flights. She went off call at 8:00 a. m., so she had the morning and most of the afternoon free. A part time morning job was just what she needed to fill those empty hours.

She had an interview with Charles Harding and his son, Rick, owners of the oil company. Here she was again with those old, conditioned ideas pulling at her. "Will they hire someone as short as I am?" She didn't need to worry. She started to work as Mr. Harding's secretary the next morning at 9:00.

She again faced another learning curve. She had had a very impressive and painful learning experience eight years before when she started with Jet East. She had learned the lesson well. This time she was gentle with herself and learned what she could one day at a time. She refused to make it important, instead enjoying the work, even if she couldn't do it perfectly the first time. Charlie was a superb and patient teacher. He complimented her when she got it right, and gently nudged her to do it over when her work fell short. And best of all, taking the elevator from the eighth floor to the second floor took her only a minute to get to work.

Life was fun.

Chapter 34

We can live without conflict.

In 1995 Jet East was sold to a competitor. She was faced with several options. She could stay on at Jet East, essentially as a new hire; she could go to another charter company; or she could move back to the Lake. It really didn't matter. She knew she could be happy, no matter what she was doing or where she was living. She now knew she was responsible for her inner state. No job or environment or situation could make her unhappy, or happy, unless she allowed it. She had carefully observed that the only time she was unhappy or upset was when something didn't go her way. Who was she to think that she would always have things her way? That was nonsense. It was also unrealistic.

All she had to do was lower her expectations and change her purpose for living. Unconsciously she had decided she deserved being comfortable. So when discomfort came along, as it always did, she didn't like it. She would try to change it, ignore it, control it, blame someone for it, complain about it and generally be in a state of conflict. She could see this attitude was destructive. As long as she lived in a body, there would always be some discomfort. That was the reality.

Discomfort, or resistance to what is, was a gift. Life had only one purpose for her--to evolve her into a conscious person. So the discomfort was a signal to her that she was operating from a misconception. Weed out the misconception and the conflict dissolved. Her misconception had been that she had a right to be

148

comfortable. As soon as she understood this misconception, she was able to enthusiastically embrace resistance and discomfort. She was free to experience everything that came her way. Whether she liked it or not, had nothing to do with it. It was going to happen anyway, so she might as well experience it gracefully. She didn't have to waste energy or time trying to arrange things to fit her idea of what life ought to be. She didn't have to wait for the ideal job, or house, or relationship to be okay. Nothing needed to be changed. Everything was okay, just as it was.

She was sixty-three years old. Maybe it was time to quit this work, work, work. She applied at several charter operators and had an interview with one. She set a salary in her head she would need in order to stay in Dallas and let the chips fall where they may. By the end of June she knew she would go back to the Lake.

Tanya and Wesley helped her move home. Harrison rode in his cage on the front seat. It didn't take him long to learn how to balance his weight so he wouldn't fall off his perch when the car turned a corner. The temperature was 103 degrees when they finished packing the U-haul truck and headed for Whitney. She sensed the door slowly closing on the wonderful life and jobs and friends she had in Dallas. She knew this new phase would be just as wonderful and fun as she allowed it to be.

When they arrived at the house, her thoughtful bridge friends had left sandwiches, salad and cookies on the bar, knowing that all of them would be hot and tired when they got in.

There was work and cleaning to be done on the house. She had the entire inside painted white along with new white carpet and drapes. She hired some of the work done. A lot of it, such as papering, caulking, cleaning windows, she did herself, provided it didn't interfere with a bridge game.

Chapter 35

Aging is a chronic disorder.

One of the greatest challenges Donna faced over the past few years was dealing with the slow, chronic illness commonly called aging. Most of her life she had been able to adapt and function with very few physical limitations. Her body was changing. The skin was losing its tone. Wrinkles silently emerged here and there. Her energy level was different. Only Donna didn't want to admit that her body was slowly but surely disintegrating. She had always had good health. Illness was foreign and repulsive. She knew anger, boredom, anxiety, fear, resentment, depression and all the negative emotions produced chemicals that the body was not equipped to handle. The body, therefore, had to adapt to these toxic emotions. The adaptation was called illness. To stay healthy she had to be free of these destructive states. She had done this to the best of her ability. For the most part, her inner state was upbeat and enthusiastic. Yet the disintegration of the body continued. She was puzzled.

Some of her friends were investing in face-lifts and tummy tucks. After thinking about it for over a year, she decided to check it out. She called for an appointment with a plastic surgeon in Waco. The receptionist said that an evaluation would be $80.

"That's all right. When do you have an appointment?"

A date was set. She took a bath and began dressing for the interview. She had been wearing some black socks around the house, which were covered with white paint. They fit perfectly in her boots, so she wore them. The doctor was only going to look at her face, anyway. She also needed to shave her legs, but who would see them? Off she went to Waco. When she jumped up on the examining table the doctor pointed at her legs and asked,

"How did this happen?"

"I have a congenital deformity. There are no knee joints. No tibia or fibula. No hip joints, only muscle and tissue. I have no ball and socket connecting the pelvis and femur," Donna explained.

"Do you mind if I take a look?"

Dirty socks. Hairy legs. "Of course not," she offered.

He was fascinated from a physician's standpoint.

He then evaluated her face. He suggested removing the puffiness from over and under the eyes.

"How much money are we talking about?" Donna asked. When she was given the cost, she said. "I'll think about it and let you know."

He guided her to the appointment desk and told his secretary, "Anytime Donna calls for her surgery, work her in."

Donna turned to leave. The secretary told her to leave by a different door.

"But I haven't paid my bill?" she protested.

"The doctor has marked your chart 'no charge' today."

The price of surgery was too high. Hadn't her life been about realizing that the outward form, the body, is only a house to live in? The real Essence, the real Being was only encased in this miraculous instrument, the body. Changing the shape and looks of the face wouldn't change that Essence.

She remembered Harrison and the aging she saw him experience. He wasn't as active as he aged. He spent less time on his swing and more time taking naps. It took more energy for him to fly up to his perches. She had never heard him complain or whine about age. A facelift? It had never occurred to him. His attitude toward life was one of total acceptance. His little mind had not accumulated a lifetime of conditioned ideas about death and dying. This left him free to experience each day to the fullest. He had no preconceived ideas how life ought to be. He probably had various aches and pains, which he took for granted. He would not let those irritations diminish his joy of living. He had not made the basic decision at his moment of birth as humans do that the purpose of living was to be comfortable. He had no ideals or illusions to live up to that would destroy his body. He was fourteen years old when he died.

She began looking for the things she could do. Her total state of health involved only four aspects: activity, environment, nutrition, and inner feeling. Activity? Shuffling cards exercised her fingers. That was about it. She bought the book, *Yoga for Dummies*, and worked for an hour each morning on the positions she could do. Yoga not only stretched the body, but it was also helpful in practicing present moment attention, which seems to be all there is.

Even though push-ups were not a Yoga routine, she did them regularly. A lot of her activities demanded she use her arms. It was vital to keep them strong. She lifted herself into the car, onto the commode, into a chair, up and down stairs. Each time she lifted her body, which was many times a day, she lifted 75 pounds. The hardest part was to keep interested in doing the exercises. The tricky mind would invent hundreds of reasons to justify skipping a day, or two: She didn't have enough time; she didn't feel like it; it was too cold, or hot; missing one day wouldn't matter, etc. This inertia or resistance was self-defeating. She knew she would do only that which she valued. At this point she put great value on having a healthy body. But sometimes the resolve was not enough to drag her out of the chair onto the Yoga pad. Yet she knew if she just did it, she would feel better physically. She would also feel better about herself.

She watched the ducks sitting on the Lake. When they started to fly out of the water it took tremendous energy to break through the surface tension of the water. Once they were free of it, they soared effortlessly. They didn't sit there waiting for a better day when it would be easier or when they had more energy. They just pushed right through it. Her motto became: *Don't think about it, Do it!*

Nutrition? This area needed some attention. While she was wearing the artificial legs, she had limited her water consumption because it wasn't always simple or easy to go to the bathroom. She could change this now. Food had not been one of her priorities. Hunger was not a driving force. She could eat or not eat. Eating cottage cheese from the container because it was quick and easy would have to go. Only she was responsible for her nutrition. She had to make a decision to provide her body with adequate fuel.

To learn more about this she went to the Optimum Health Institute in Austin for two weeks, where she learned to eat better. They suggested no cooked foods because enzymes are destroyed at around 117 degrees. No sugar. No bread. No dairy products. No supplements. No caffeine. No meat. Although she didn't stay on this strict of a diet, she did eat more raw fruits and vegetables. She avoided meat, bread, dairy products and sugar most of the time. It was certainly a worthwhile education. However, caffeine remained her drug of choice.

Environment? Her physical environment couldn't have been nicer. Her house overlooked Lake Whitney and the area was quiet and peaceful. "Perhaps though, I live in that which I radiate." She took a long look at the energy she radiated around her and concluded that it was environmentally safe. Her accumulation of plants, some thirty-five of them were happy and healthy. That should tell her something.

Inner feelings? Donna knew negative emotions were destructive to her body. These emotions produced chemicals that were destructive to the body at a cellular level. She could check this out. She had noticed when she was upset, angry, or in a snit, that within 72 hours there would be a physical adaptation of some kind. She would have a headache, rash, runny nose, upset stomach, back ache or other irritations. When her attitude was one of peace and joy, the body would work quite harmoniously. She simply could not afford negative emotions.

She simply could not afford to resist aging anymore. Resisting it would only speed up the process.

Chapter 36

We are spiritual beings having human experiences.

The beautiful carved artificial legs she wore for 32 years are now tucked snugly under the bed. Although it would take some practice, she can return to the tall world anytime she wants to. She hesitates to throw them away because they are irreplaceable. She even has some stylish, but outdated, clothes left over from her tall years. There is no longing or yearning to be tall again. She has no desire to be any different than what she is. The conflict is gone. Occasionally, she has dressed up tall for fun, sometimes to enliven a dull party.

She now knows she is a privileged invited guest on this beautiful estate called Earth at an incredible Party put on by the Host called Life. This must be a Party. When there is a bunch of people together playing games it's called a Party. She arrived at the Party helpless, naked, toothless and unable to speak the language. She had two slaves to take care of her. Ever since she arrived at the Party, the Host has provided her abundantly with everything she has needed for the past 69 years. She has had clothes to wear, a home to live in, a car to drive, food to eat, interesting things to do and interesting people to be around. What more could she want? She has it all.

Because she is so thankful to be invited to this incredible Party there might be something she could do to express her gratitude to the Host for inviting her. She does this by being considerate and harmless to the other guests, herself and the Planet. She also understands that she makes a contribution to Life by expressing a harmonious mood, wherever she goes. She does not do this 100 per cent of the time, but realizes it's a worthy purpose to aim for.

Perhaps in these troubled times of 2002 that may be the most valuable contribution she can make for all of Mankind.

To order additional copies of *The Short and Tall of It*

Name _____

Address _____

_____

$14.95 x _____ copies =   _____

Sales Tax   _____
(Texas residents add 8.25% sales tax)

Please add $3.50 postage and handling per book   _____

Total amount due: _____

Please send check or money order for books to:

Word Wright International
P.O. Box 1785
Georgetown, TX 78627

For a complete listing of Word Wright International books, check out our
website at http://www.wordwright.biz

Printed in the United States
19031LVS00005B/205-207